OFF-PISTE
PERFORMANCE

Alison Thacker

First published in Great Britain 2025 by Pesda Press
Tan y Coed Canol
Ceunant
Caernarfon
Gwynedd
LL55 4RN

© Copyright 2025 Alison Thacker

ISBN: 978-1-906095-94-9

The Author has asserted her rights under the Copyright, Designs and Patents Act, 1988, to be identified as Author of this Work. All rights reserved. No part of this publication may be reproduced, stored in a retrieval system, or transmitted, in any form or by any means, electronic, mechanical, photocopying, recording or otherwise, without the prior written permission of the publisher.

Printed in Poland, www.lfbookservices.co.uk

Front cover photo: off-piste skiing in the Aiguilles Rouge, Chamonix. © Daniel Wildey

Kath Thow enjoying summit to sea powder conditions on an untracked mountain above the Norwegian fjords.

CONTENTS

Acknowledgements	6
About the author	8
Photo credits	9
Introduction	11

GOING OFF-PISTE — 13
What is off-piste skiing?	14
My approach	16
How to use this book	17
Safety	20
Off-piste skiing grades	21

PREPARATION — 23
Physical	25
Psychological	26
Equipment	27
Environment	38
Warm up	40
Practice on the hill	42

ESSENTIAL SKILLS — 43
Static skills	43
Movement skills	51

KEY MOVEMENTS — 61
Balancing over the outside ski	62
Bending and stretching	68
Moving forward into the turn	73

TURNING — 81
Twisting	83
Edging	87

DIFFERENT TYPES OF SNOW — 91
Hard packed snow	92
Spring snow	95
Icy snow	97
Powder	99
Chopped-up powder	105
Heavy snow	108
Crust	114

TERRAIN VARIATIONS — 119
Steep	120
Convex	127
Concave	129
Bumps	130
Narrow	134
Trees	138
Paths	141

COMBINING SNOW AND TERRAIN VARIATIONS — 143

POOR VISIBILITY — 147

ADDITIONAL SKILLS — 151
Half turns	151
Jump turns	153
Double pole plant	160
Baton ramasse	160
Small drops	161
Downhill kick turns	164

COMMONLY ASKED QUESTIONS — 167

INDEX — 182

ACKNOWLEDGEMENTS

I hope that you find this book a useful resource on your off-piste skiing journey. I am exceedingly grateful to all those people that have played a part in my own skiing journey, that led me to a place where I was able to put my spoken words into a book.

Thank you to all those who 'taught me to ski' right from my first moments sliding down the local golf course, to the race coaches and trainers who helped me to progress through the BASI system. Many of their words to me are reflected in my teaching today and I still hear their voices in my head when developing my own ski performance. (Mum and Dad, Ali Anderson, Keith Morris, Graeme Nesbit, Duncan Barton, Hugh Clark, John Clark, Bruce Cranston, Ali Rainback, Zoe Campbell, Derek Tate). Without snow, I would never have learned to ski, so thank you to the late James McIntosh, his family and staff at The Lecht Ski Centre for continually moving snow around to ensure there was enough to get me hooked on the sport. There are numerous others who may not be aware they have taught me to ski, but everybody that I have had the pleasure to ski with has taught me something, made me question an idea or an explanation, or given me skiing to observe. Whether the perceived relationship has been that of coach / student or equals, learning has taken place.

I am incredibly grateful for the continued support from Shona and Derek Tate. Derek assessed me on my BASI teaching course and then they invited me to come and teach with them in Chamonix, which turned out to be a life-changing opportunity. Thank you to Bruce Goodlad for giving me the opportunity to write a chapter in his book, which planted the seed that there might be scope for a book dedicated to off-piste ski technique.

For a while, I found myself resisting nudges from the people I skied with to write down what I was teaching on the hill. Eventually, their gentle persuasion got the better of me and I started to commit words to paper. I doubt that this project would have ever been completed if it wasn't for the words of encouragement from Hannah Hollinger, unknowingly offering a few simple words of advice, at exactly the right time, which enabled me to embrace the writing process.

ACKNOWLEDGEMENTS

Thank you to Sue Savege, Sarah Dunn and Susie and Dougal Ranford for reading early drafts and offering honest feedback in the initial stages. I am indebted to Susie Ranford for her extended proof reading, suggested edits and making a significant contribution to the final version of this book. I'm not sure I would have got to the finished product without this help! Rachel Bracha let me know that she'd find typos in the finished version, so kindly offered to find them before and read my final draft which I am incredibly grateful for. Kris Hill generously gave his time to produce the diagrams in this book, which brought meaning to my tentatively hand drawn sketches. Thank you to Franco at Pesda Press for taking on my project and being understanding as life gave many delays. All errors are mine and as I continue on my skiing journey, I am sure that my thoughts and ideas will develop, and I am happy for them to be challenged to promote further growth and improvements.

Thank you to my sister Gillian for being available for Auntie duties to make time to write the book. I am extremely grateful to my husband James for taking on more than his share of household tasks to allow the time and space for this book to come to fruition and for spending late nights searching through catalogues of photos, often for a specific image that I vaguely remembered being taken many years ago! I'm now looking forward to having more time available for skiing together again, and starting our daughter Abigail on her skiing journey.

This book would not have been possible, or needed, if it wasn't for you, the reader and skier, seeking to improve your off-piste performance, and for that opportunity I am incredibly grateful. You have given me the opportunity to observe reoccurring themes but also see the diversity of individuals' styles. I hope that this book helps you to develop your off-piste performance further and maximise your enjoyment from the sport.

Alison Thacker

ABOUT THE AUTHOR

Alison Thacker started skiing aged two and trained as a child and teenager with the Gordon Skiers, representing both Scotland and Great Britain internationally. At 20 she gained the highest level of BASI ski instructor award, at the time one of the youngest people to do so. After achieving a First-Class Honours degree in Outdoor Studies at Ambleside, Alison moved to Chamonix where she lived and worked for 15 years as a ski instructor in winter and a walking leader in summer. During this period, she started running popular off-piste ski courses, later founding the specialist ski training and guiding business Off-Piste Performance, as well as a company delivering Duke of Edinburgh training and assessment expeditions for schools. Alison continues to run both businesses successfully from her home in Kingussie, in the Scottish Highlands, where she lives with her husband James, an IFMGA Mountain Guide, and their daughter Abigail.

PHOTO CREDITS

This book would have been nothing without the use of suitable imagery to accompany the text. I have been fortunate to be able to work with professional photographers on this project, whose skill in skiing made this job so much easier as they already had an eye for what I was looking for. I am incredibly grateful for the patience of Daniel Wildey, for putting up with me saying, 'Can we do that once more', not just on one photo shoot, but two, after I decided that I looked far too pregnant in the photos from the first one, some of which did make the final cut for the book. Thanks to Fiona Morrison for being Daniel's assistant on our final photo shoot, and pointing out my errors! Thanks to Olly Bowman for committing to a day before I informed him that what I needed was 'shots of skiing in bad snow', when we spent the morning skiing all the snow that others were avoiding. Thanks to Paul Mason for being available at short notice to help with the equipment shots, and to Hamish and his team at Cairngorm Mountain Sports in Aviemore for giving us the use of their space and equipment.

Thank you to all those who were happy for me to use their images: Claire Bennet, Bruce Goodlad, Di Gilbert, Tom Hill, Paul "Skinny" Jones, Gregor Mcllenan, George Reid, Jim Savege, Alan Scowcroft, Rachel Spraggs, James Thacker, Alistair Todd, Andy Townsend, Kelly VanderBeek, BASI and La Clinque du Sport.

I am greatly appreciative of those who let me use images of them skiing, as I am sure the readers are, as in so many cases a picture speaks a thousand words. Thanks to Julie Bernasconi, Tim Blakemore, Mike Brownlow, Rich Cross, John Dudley, John Evans, Andy Fyfe, Barbara Gibbons, Di Gilbert, Penny Granger, Kenny Grant, Phil Griffiths, Richard Hammond, Jon Hettle, Julia Hobson, Dave Hollinger, Susan Hurst, Neil and Max Johnson, Emma Lawrenson, Neil Maclean-Martin, Amy Marwick, Lynn Mill, Izzy Milne, Fiona Morrison, Rob Muir, Andy Nelson, Gillian Parker, Susie Ranford, George Reid, Dave Rudkin, Jim Savege, Alan Scowcroft, Ewan Stewart, James Thacker and Kath Thow. Thanks to Sandy Houston for his kind permission to use a photo of the late Susan Houston.

James Thacker exploring some of the steeper terrain on Ben Nevis, Scotland.
Jim Savege

INTRODUCTION

This book is about developing off-piste skiing performance so that skiers can travel more efficiently in the mountains and gain more enjoyment from the sport. It looks at essential skills, discusses key movements which are transferable from piste skiing, and looks at how these are varied depending on the ever-changing terrain and snow types. It is not a definitive manual, rather an exploration of ideas and themes which will form part of any skiers' learning journey.

PARTICIPATION STATEMENT

The author and the publisher recognise that off-piste skiing is a sport with a risk of injury, or death. Participants in off-piste skiing should be aware of and accept these risks and take responsibility for their own actions.

GOING OFF-PISTE

Embracing some challenging snow conditions on steeper terrain (photo ▲).
📷 Olly Bowman Photography

Enjoying some easy angled powder skiing (photo ◀).
📷 Daniel Wildey

Off-piste skiing in The Dolomites (photo ▼), Scotland (photo ◢) and Norway (photo ▶).

Off-piste skiing, a sport unique to the winter mountains, draws participants for many different reasons. The lure of off-piste skiing may be the challenge of physical activity, the buzz of speed, to explore new areas, to escape the crowds, for mental focus, to journey efficiently in the mountains in winter, or simply the sensation of executing the perfect turn. Whatever the aspiration, poor technique can leave off-piste skiers feeling tired, frustrated, and exposed to the risk of injury. In contrast, perform skilfully and you will save energy, be less prone to injury, have heightened enjoyment, and feel motivated and inspired to do more. This book aims to help all off-piste skiers (and those with a desire to become one) with downhill ski technique, whether it be your first time venturing outside of the piste markers or if you are an experienced ski mountaineer wishing to refine your techniques.

OFF-PISTE PERFORMANCE

WHAT IS OFF-PISTE SKIING?

Off-piste skiing is a winter sport best described as skiing that takes place away from marked ski runs. Marked ski runs are controlled and managed, and are most commonly defined by coloured marker poles down either side of the slope. When skiing within the marker poles, you are on-piste. When skiing outside of the marker poles, you are off-piste.

Off-piste skiing could take place just outside of the marker poles, but equally it could be in Antarctica, away from civilisation and ski lifts. Front country, side country and backcountry are non-specific terms used to informally describe off-piste ski environments, indicating how remote the off-piste skiing is from any marked ski runs. Whatever your interpretation of each of these terms, they all encompass off-piste skiing. Ski touring and ski mountaineering, where skins are used to ascend, both involve an element of off-piste skiing. As do freeriding and extreme skiing. Off-piste skiing isn't new, although arguably it has gained popularity with recent developments in equipment. At one time, all skiing was 'off-piste'. When marker poles and piste machines arrived, so did the term off-piste.

Many skiers find that off-piste skiing becomes their true passion as it allows them a form of self-expression and physical and mental challenges away from any constraints or perceived boundaries.

Off-piste skiing is involved in all the below activities, from being just outside of the marked ski runs to being on a remote ski mountaineering expedition.

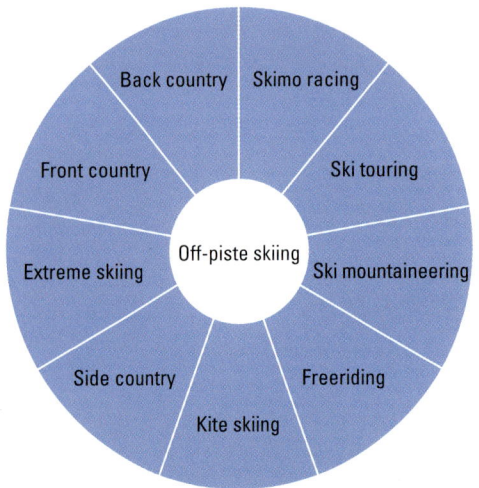

The skiers in the foreground are off-piste, with pistes and ski lifts visible in the background.

GOING OFF-PISTE

Powder 'off-piste' conditions on a marked run, within the ski area boundary (photo ▲).

'Piste' conditions, with smooth grippy snow, outside of the marked ski runs (photo ◥).

It is often presumed that skiing off-piste means skiing powder in the depths of winter, and a velvety blanket of spring snow towards the end of the season. Unfortunately, this is not always the case, particularly if it has not snowed for many weeks. Instead, off-piste skiing encompasses every snow type that the weather and mountain can generate. An off-piste skier needs to become effective at skiing all snow types and terrain features.

When skiing between the marker poles it is sometimes assumed that the slopes will be pisted or groomed, having been smoothed by a machine. However, it is not unheard of to find snow conditions which are typical of off-piste, on the piste. This is common when there is a big fall of snow early in the morning without time for the runs to be pisted before opening. The deep powder found on-piste can quickly become bumpy due to the high volume of people skiing within a defined corridor, resulting in challenging 'off-piste' ski conditions within the confines of the marked ski runs. This is why an off-piste skillset can be beneficial even for those who don't intend to venture outside of the marker poles, and will lead to becoming a more diverse and accomplished skier, irrespective of where you wish to ski. It is also an excellent training opportunity to become familiar with different snow types, without having to worry about the additional hazards of skiing outside of the marked runs.

Conversely, 'piste' conditions can sometimes be found beyond the marked ski runs. This occurs most frequently when the wind has stripped any fresh snow away, resulting in a smooth, hard-packed, uniform surface to ski on.

It would be wrong to presume that when going off-piste skiing automatically becomes more challenging. This is not always the case. There are times when skiing off-piste is easier than skiing in between the marker poles. This can occur when pistes become icy through increased traffic and the snow off-piste is still firm and grippy. Also, this could be because the pistes are crowded and there is more space for skiing off-piste.

MY APPROACH

My philosophy is that off-piste skiing is about going from A to B safely, efficiently and having as much fun as possible, whatever the conditions. There are many ways in which this can be achieved and what works for one person, may not work for another. At the heart of what I teach is the skier as an individual. I believe that any skier can go off-piste with the correct guidance and approach. In terms of technical skiing, the marker poles are often more of a perceived boundary than an actual one.

My thoughts and ideas have been developed over many years of seeing reoccurring themes and I strive to use simple, yet effective, language for potentially complex situations. I believe that there is often one solution to many problems, and equally, there can be many solutions to one problem. I have no intention for skiing to be learned solely from a book. Learning should be a holistic process, acknowledging that people learn in different ways. I believe and hope that this book will be part of the learning and development process for many.

Rather than perfecting individual techniques or turn types, I believe in blending appropriate movements for the desired outcome, leading to infinite possibilities. I prefer to think of movements rather than fixed positions. I'm reluctant to believe in 'bad habits'. More often it's a case of the wrong habit for the situation that results in ineffective performance. For example, a skier might perceive that they have a bad habit of facing their shoulders across the hill but, in some situations, this is a positive attribute. I encourage understanding when your 'habits' will help your performance, and learning some new 'habits' for the situations you find challenging. However, there are a few situations where I find myself saying "Don't do that", as the risk of injury is high, and these potential pitfalls are highlighted throughout the book.

In my view, all of the performance components (physical, psychological, equipment, environment, technical and tactical), which are discussed briefly in the next chapter, are of equal importance. However, the focus of this book is on the technical and tactical aspects as that is where my expertise and interest lie.

Alison teaching a few new habits.

I hope that skiers enjoy the feel of skiing and develop an understanding of what feels effective, being less concerned by how their skiing looks. By developing an understanding of what feels good, we become able to respond to feedback that we get from the skis and the snow.

I believe that strong performances come through dedicated, appropriate and structured practice with clear end goals. But don't get bogged down, remember what it is all about. Take a moment to look around, enjoy the place that you are aiming to travel more efficiently in and enjoy the sensation of that perfect turn.

HOW TO USE THIS BOOK

This book is aimed at anyone who wants to improve their downhill off-piste skiing performance, whether it be the first time away from the piste markers, through to highly experienced off-piste skiers looking to develop their skills. It may also be useful to those who wish to offer guidance to other skiers. The book aims to use simple language and steers away from using technical terms, although reference is sometimes made to other terminology. It is hoped that it will be read with an open mind, by skiers who want to make changes.

It can be argued that skiing can't be learnt from a book. While that view holds some truth, this book would not exist if it wasn't thought to be of great benefit to all skiers. However, it must be acknowledged that this book is only part of the picture and it hasn't been written to be used in isolation. It should be used as a tool to aid progression alongside other learning methods such as plenty of purposeful practice, lessons and video analysis.

This book can be used in different ways. It can be used as preparation before undertaking lessons, or as a resource to refer back to after lessons and individual practice sessions. It can be used as a reminder of key points at the beginning of the season and as a reference book; referring to individual chapters when required. The book can be read from cover to cover, but there will be more value in referring to one element at a time, reflecting, practising, and coming back to it again. The book highlights the need to constantly change and adapt in order to be skilful in the constantly changing environment. It is not exhaustive. We are all different shapes and sizes and some adaptations will be unique to you. It is hoped that by reading the book, you will be more proficient at making changes and will be able to experiment to find solutions specific to you, so that you ski more efficiently and enjoyably.

Throughout the book are quotes from a diverse range of learners, from first-timers off-piste to ski instructors and mountain guides. These are their 'light bulb moments' when an aspect of off-piste skiing made sense for them, significant learning took place, and there was a huge leap forward in their off-piste technical development. It is hoped that these can be of use to other skiers, as they reinforce the key points and demonstrate where they have been put into practice on the mountain.

These are additional sections of information that might be of interest to some readers, and delve a little deeper into some subject areas that are mentioned briefly in the text.

Throughout the book there are a variety of different drills to practise on the hill. The drills are also good warm-up exercises.

These indicate significant points that will have an impact on safety and could result in injury.

OFF-PISTE PERFORMANCE

> "If I struggled off-piste, I used to find myself doing more of the same, thinking I wasn't doing enough and just needed to do more, do it better, do it stronger. I now know that if it's not working, I need to make a change. To a certain extent, it doesn't matter what that initial change is, but I need to try something different."

The underlying ethos of this book is about using techniques and tactics to improve and maintain control when skiing off-piste. Control is the core of skiing. Control allows the skier to journey and travel. That control is across two dimensions: speed and direction. Generally, a skier will feel satisfied with their performance if they have gone where they want to (control of direction) and if they have travelled at the speed they want to (control of speed). In an optimum performance, the skier will have dictated the speed and direction. To achieve this off-piste, constant changes are required. Just as it feels that control has been mastered, the snow type may change and suddenly the next turn has not been executed as planned. In the off-piste environment, it is critical to regain control as quickly and efficiently as possible.

First, the Preparation chapter looks briefly at factors that can improve ski performance away from developing technical skills on snow. Essential Skills describes skills that are vital for skiing off-piste. Key Movements looks at movements that are transferable from piste skiing and have a huge impact on performance when skiing off-piste. The more familiarity and skill there is with these movements, the more they can be exaggerated and varied according to the terrain. Time spent ensuring these are well-dialled on-piste, will be time well spent. Turning describes two distinctly different ways of turning the skis, which can then be blended to adapt to the conditions. The book then looks at how to vary these key movements and turns for different types of snow and terrain, also taking into account poor visibility. Additional Skills covers tools which can further enhance performance and enjoyment. Lastly, the book has a chapter of Commonly Asked Questions. These mostly provide short answers and refer back to descriptions and drills in earlier sections of the book.

When skiers are confronted with a challenging situation, performance tends to drop as movements become inhibited. For example, if bending and stretching of the legs is required to absorb bumps, less bending and stretching tends to occur when faced with large bumps on a steep slope. Yet this is precisely the time when the movements need to be enhanced! In these challenging situations, when movements might be inhibited, envisage that you are likely to do about 50% of your movement potential, when in fact 100% would be optimal. Therefore, extensive practice with exaggerated movements is hugely beneficial. Practise with 150% and then 100% will occur when the movement is really needed.

Practising drills is an excellent way to exaggerate movement patterns and help the movements to become ingrained. Do the drills to develop the skills.

Performing drills both on and off-piste.

To gain maximum benefit, once rehearsed on-piste, drills should also be practised in a dynamic environment with constantly changing variables to make them directly relevant to off-piste skiing.

The difficulty level of all the drills can be increased in similar ways. The difficulty can be increased by any of the following methods or a combination of them, but ideally not all at once:

- Increase the gradient of the slope.
- Increase the speed at which the drill is being performed.
- Change the terrain / snow type.
- Challenge balance, e.g. do the drill without poles, with boots undone or with eyes shut.
- Add a competitive element to the drill.

If the drill is to be done without poles, and it's not possible to leave your poles at the bottom of the slope, they can be carried between your rucksack's straps.

If the drill can be achieved first time, then the level of challenge needs to be increased. The difficulty level should be increased gradually to a point where the drill is not easy and where you are initially unsuccessful at it, but the challenge is not too great, such that there is no hope of success. Drills are also a worthwhile way to spend time when the weather is bad or there are only a few runs open.

Storing poles for doing drills without poles.

"Every season I give myself the goal of trying to be successful at a drill that, at the start of the season, I cannot do. I'll try and have a little practice every time I go skiing, even if only for 5 minutes. Last season, the goal was to be able to ski on one ski by the end of the season. Not only did this keep me motivated when conditions were sub-optimal, but it also gave me concrete evidence that I was becoming a better skier, which in turn boosted my morale and motivation."

OFF-PISTE PERFORMANCE

A word on photos

There are numerous photos throughout the book. The majority of photos highlight good movements. However, in a few cases, photos have been used to illustrate poor technique, which are the few things that could be classed as 'bad habits', where there is a likelihood of falling or risk of injury. For clarity, these have a red cross next to them.

Many of the photos have been taken on-piste so that the feet and skis can be seen clearly.

While photos are used here to illustrate key points, it is not recommended to use photographs as a way to analyse your own performance. Plenty of bad photos are taken to get one good one! Video is a much better alternative as it shows the movement rather than a still position.

SAFETY

The complete off-piste skill set extends far beyond efficient downhill technique. Off-piste skiing can be a hazardous activity and appropriate steps need to be taken to reduce the associated risks. Steps taken will include:

- Checking the weather forecast for the area.
- Checking the avalanche forecast for the area.
- Developing an appropriate level of avalanche awareness and avalanche rescue knowledge.
- Having the knowledge and equipment to navigate in the winter mountain environment, away from marked runs.
- Checking local reports of conditions via resources such as ski patrol, websites and social media feeds.
- Carrying the necessary equipment.
- Knowing how to raise the alarm for rescue.
- Ensuring you have the appropriate skill level for the chosen location. This may involve undertaking training courses in mountain safety.
- Developing knowledge of the terrain (specialised equipment and skills are required for skiing on a glacier).
- Developing knowledge of the non-technical skills that underpin sound decision-making.

Avalanche hazard information displayed within a ski resort (photo ▼).

Numerous mountain skills are required for skiing safely off-piste. This book only covers technique for descending off-piste (photo ▶).

GOING OFF-PISTE

These safety aspects are outside the scope of this book as they are comprehensive subjects in their own right. They are covered in detail in Bruce Goodlad's book *Ski Touring: Essential knowledge for off-piste, back country, ski tourers and ski mountaineers*. It is recommended to undertake a winter mountain safety course before venturing off-piste for the first time and undertaking regular training to ensure your skills are current. Consider hiring an IFMGA Mountain Guide or suitably qualified ski instructor when skiing off-piste, particularly if skiing in a new area or undertaking objectives that exceed your current skill set.

Safety is of paramount importance and an important factor to consider when creating a suitable environment for learning. For example, you should not be worrying about where your off-piste run is going or if the snow conditions are stable, while trying to focus on technical development. Distractions need to be limited in order to be open to absorbing new techniques and to focus on practice. Addressing safety factors will significantly reduce many potential distractions. The key is to ensure safety factors are addressed, not ignored.

OFF-PISTE SKIING GRADES

Pisted runs are allocated colours to indicate their level of difficulty, ranging from green (easy) through to black (difficult). This is the usual approach although it is not standardised across all ski resorts. There is no such system for off-piste skiing. Due to the dynamic nature of the environment, an off-piste run that seems easy one day might become more challenging in different snow and weather conditions. Some organisations, guidebooks and map publications have developed their own grading system for off-piste runs. This is helpful for planning when comparisons are made within one system.

Strava and its grading system (photo ▼).

Vamos guidebook for L'Alpe D'Huez, Les Deux Alpes and La Grave (photo ▶).

A good example of this is Strava, an app for planning, recording and discovering outdoor sports. Strava has its own grading system for off-piste ski runs, giving a rating for difficulty, exposure and remoteness, alongside detailed mapping with a gradient overlay.

Vamos produces an excellent set of guidebooks with English translations for the off-piste areas within, and close to, the major French ski resorts. These have a grading system for difficulty and seriousness.

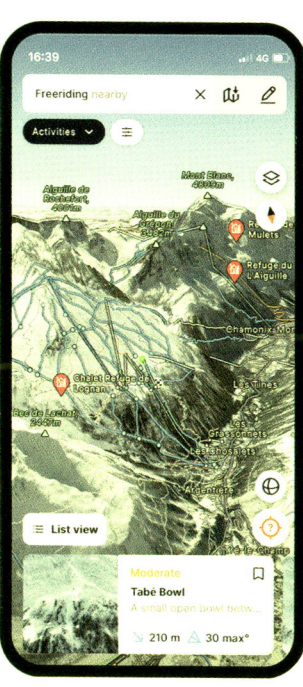

OFF-PISTE PERFORMANCE

Skiing in La Grave, lift-accessed off-piste skiing.

In some ski areas itinerary runs are marked on the piste maps. These are runs that are marked with poles and are controlled for safety but are not pisted. Itinerary runs are a good way to develop off-piste ski techniques within the confines of a managed area.

There are also a number of ski lifts which access areas with no marked pistes, leaving the majority of the ski area wild and natural. These are unique, command respect, and need to be treated as unmanaged off-piste. A good example of this is La Grave in France, which has become legendary as an off-piste skier's paradise. Here there are routes but not runs. These should only be embarked on with proficient downhill technique and all of the skills listed in the safety section, or alternatively, with an IFMGA Mountain Guide.

It is essential to find the right slope for the desired level of challenge or practice, and to recognise that conditions on this slope will change from day to day, or even hour to hour.

PREPARATION

Discussing the prevailing conditions while getting ready and ensuring boots are fitting well.

Preparation is key to success in any sport. There are a number of things to do before setting foot on the mountain to give yourself the best chance of success. There are six key components to improving sporting performance. These are all applicable to off-piste ski performance, each needing significant attention. The *BASI Manual* refers to these as the performance threads:

- Physical
- Psychological
- Equipment
- Environment
- Technical
- Tactical

The focus of this book is on the technical and tactical components. Specialists such as psychologists, sports scientists, dieticians, ski technicians, boot fitters and fitness trainers are best placed to look at the other components. However, as these components influence each other, it is important that all are mentioned briefly within the context of this book. While each component should be understood in isolation, it is essential to see how they become interlinked and overlap. Incremental performance improvements arc gained from developing across all components.

Imagine that you wish to ski short rhythmical turns in deep powder (tactical). You have small baskets on the ends of the ski poles (equipment). Every time you plant your pole it sinks deep into the snow, knocking you off balance (technical). You become increasingly frustrated by this (psychological). You change the baskets of the poles to large powder baskets (equipment). Now your pole plant aids balance (technical). In turn, you are able to execute short rhythmical turns (tactical) and as a result, your confidence increases (psychological).

Another example is when the wind is much stronger than expected (environment). You feel cold (physical) so hunch your shoulders and bury your face in your jacket to try and keep warm. You wish you had put on more layers this morning (equipment). You feel stiff (physical) and your movements on skis feel forced and robotic. You find yourself accelerating out of the end of the turn (technical) and don't feel in control from one turn to the next. You feel frustrated that you can't keep up with your friends (psychological). You go to the café to warm up (physical) and put on some extra layers (equipment). The wind decreases (environment). Your legs now bend and stretch fluidly through their full range of movement (technical), resulting in control from one turn to the next. You are now in front of your friends as you feel more assertive (psychological) and they are following your line (tactical).

Short-term and long-term

In both of the examples above, temporary changes to the environment, physical and equipment components have resulted in instantaneous negative and positive changes to the technical, tactical and psychological components. Good preparation will ensure a strong performance from the outset. These are examples of where the different components have had short-term influence.

It is important to highlight that sometimes a long-term approach is needed, and this is where the skills of the specialists named earlier may need to be called upon. For example, you may find that you cannot flex your ankles very much (physical) and this results in always feeling like your weight is over the backs of the skis (technical) and there is pressure on your calf muscles which can become painful. Rarely do you feel in control and skiing feels strenuous. This could be down to having boots which are too stiff (equipment). However, you also find that you are unable to flex your ankles much when not in ski boots. This may need a longer-term approach of a fitness training programme specifically for developing ankle flexion, or it may need physiotherapy to improve the range of movement in the ankle joint. These long-term changes need significant commitment and motivation, but the results can be momentous and cause vast leaps forward in skiing performance.

"I'd frequently been told to flex my ankles when skiing, always with limited success. Even after numerous drills, little progress was made. I even changed my boots to a softer model. Then I tried flexing my ankles away from skiing, without ski boots on, and there was very little movement. How could I expect to do this movement on skis, if I couldn't do it off skis! I then had a summer of regular physiotherapy and committed to the exercises that they gave me to do at home. When I returned to skis the following winter, I could flex my ankles much better and skiing felt less strenuous and became much more enjoyable"

PREPARATION

PHYSICAL

The physical component covers a wide spectrum of variables such as biomechanics, sleep patterns and diet, through to the physical fitness attributes of strength, endurance, power, flexibility, and aerobic and anaerobic fitness. Being physically prepared for skiing has three primary benefits: it reduces the risk of injury; ensures a greater level of enjoyment from a day's skiing; and it helps to make technical adjustments quickly.

Off-piste skiing has deliberately been referred to in this book as a sport, meaning an activity involving physical exertion, as opposed to recreation which refers to an activity done for enjoyment and not involving the same level of physical exertion. When skiing is viewed as recreation, this generally indicates a lower level of performance. To have success skiing off-piste, a sporting approach is required.

Are you training for a marathon or a sprint? This will depend on your approach to skiing the mountain. Do you prefer to ski short pitches in a powerful manner, or ski thousands of metres of descent without stopping? Often the mountain will dictate which is preferable, so it's best to prepare physically for both. For example, if skiing underneath seracs you don't want to linger. A good steady pace will be preferable where you can keep going without needing a rest. In contrast, when faced with a slope covered in crust, powerful movements are required and it is better to operate in short pitches. Therefore, consider training for both a marathon and a sprint-type approach.

A good place to start physical training is with some cross-training away from the snow. Climbing, hill-walking, and mountain-biking are great sports to physically train for skiing and also help with psychological and environmental preparation.

Mountain biking is an excellent sport to do in the off season, helping with both physical and psychological preparation. The movements displayed here are very similar to those discussed in the key movements chapter.

OFF-PISTE PERFORMANCE

Ski-specific exercises are a fantastic way to strengthen the muscles and fine-tune motor movements ready for the ski season, with a strong focus on the core muscles. Aim to factor these in a couple of months before the ski season starts. The BeFit app is excellent and comes highly recommended. These exercises can be as simple as taking every opportunity to balance on one leg, do some hopping and perform a few squats. Start balancing on one leg while brushing your teeth and you will feel the benefit when the ski season arrives.

Demonstrating a ski-specific exercise, which relates to the key movement of bending and stretching.
📷 *La Clinque du Sport*

PSYCHOLOGICAL

This important and complex component has a place in all sports. Training the mind for skiing is as essential as training the body. The benefits of good psychological preparation are very similar to that of physical preparation; reducing the risk of injury, improving technical performance and increasing enjoyment.

Derek Tate's book *Six Steps for Training the Mind* is an excellent resource for all skiers striving for optimal performance. It gives practical activities to help train the mind, while recognising the everyday stresses of modern-day life. The book looks at attitude, self-talk, relaxation, mental rehearsal, pre-performance routines and optimal performance.

These aspects in Derek's book can be combined with an increase in technical knowledge to bring about improved performance. For example, if you become familiar with using self-talk effectively, this can be linked to a technical or tactical focus that you know helps you to ski better. A good technical or tactical focus that you know has worked previously can redirect your attention away from any psychological fears that may inhibit performance. Simply repeating helpful key words out loud can have a direct positive influence on performance.

Skier using visualisation to help prepare for a high-level performance.
📷 *Kelly VanderBeek*

> "When my instructor asked what my aspirations for the course were, I said that I would like to get to their level, where I didn't need to think about skiing anymore. I have to admit that I was disappointed when the instructor replied saying that they were always focused when they were skiing. Then the penny dropped. Maybe the reason that I wasn't as good as I wanted to be was purely down to focus. I was skiing down slopes with the aspiration that one day I wouldn't have to worry about the bumps in front of me and would be able to think about what I was doing next week. Perhaps I wouldn't be worrying, but I would always need to be focused. Now, by staying focused on the activity, or the movements, sensations or sounds of the activity, I perform better and it is also a mental escape from the challenges of my day-to-day life. The more focused I am, the less effort skiing seems to require."

PREPARATION

Flow

In the context of skiing, there are two distinctly different meanings of 'flow' and they should not be confused. Firstly, there is what might be termed 'a flowing performance'. 'Flowing performance' is commonly used in sport and in essence is a skilful performance. In skiing, this skilful performance is being done in a complex environment. With this use, a flowing performance would be likened to the dictionary definition of "moving steadily and continuously".

Secondly, flow is referred to as a state of mind or experience, most famously defined by Csikszentmihalyi as "a state in which people are so involved in an activity that nothing else seems to matter; the experience is so enjoyable that people will continue to do it even at great cost, for the sheer sake of doing it".

Of course, these two principles can be linked as a flowing performance can lead to a state of flow, or vice versa. The benefit of linking these is that when people experience flow state and a flowing performance, the experience is much richer and more enjoyable, especially after the event, and this promotes improvement and growth.

EQUIPMENT

Having the right equipment for skiing off-piste, and ensuring it is in good working order, is crucial and will contribute towards reaching your full potential. In just the same way as the physical and psychological components, having the right equipment reduces the risk of injury, improves technical performance and increases enjoyment.

Developments in ski equipment are rapid and it is important to look at the most up-to-date information available. What follows is not an exhaustive kit list, but rather highlights key points regarding certain pieces of equipment that can have a huge impact on downhill performance. A detailed kit list can be found in Bruce Goodlad's book *Ski Touring: Essential knowledge for off-piste, back country, ski tourers and ski mountaineers*.

A selection of different skis, all suitable for off-piste skiing.

Skis

The choice of skis can be overwhelming, due to the range on offer coupled with significant advances in ski technology over recent years. Here are a few factors to consider when deciding which skis to buy.

Width underfoot

The dimensions of a ski are given by a number such as 120/90/110. The first number is the width of the ski at the front, the middle number is the width in the middle of the ski, referred to as underfoot, and the last number is the width at the tail. For off-piste skiing, most skiers will look for a ski that is over 90mm underfoot. Consider where the majority of your skiing will take place. If this is to be regularly in deep powder, then a wider ski will be beneficial as the skis will float better. Remember that off-piste encompasses everything from hardpack to powder, and

OFF-PISTE PERFORMANCE

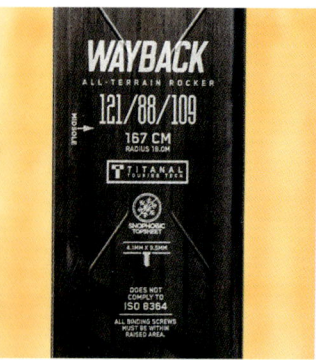

The ski dimensions are displayed on the skis.

you may spend the majority of your time with your skis on the surface of the snow even though you are off-piste. Given more mixed conditions, a ski around 90mm will be preferable. Very wide skis are for off-piste where you are primarily skiing in the snow, rather than on it.

Radius

The ski will also have a turn radius given in metres. The longer the radius, the more stable the ski will be at higher speeds. The shorter the radius, the more agile the ski, and the easier it will generally be to turn. A longer radius ski will be more challenging to turn, particularly in small spaces. A ski with a short turning radius will feel less stable at speed, particularly on firm snow, and may result in juddering. Remember that the radius will increase with the length of the ski. For example, a 170cm ski may have a radius of 17m, whereas the 177cm version of the same ski might be 19m.

Stiffness

A stiffer ski will be more stable at speed but can be harder to turn in small spaces. A flexible ski will be easier to turn in small spaces but may feel flappy when travelling at high speed, particularly when going straight.

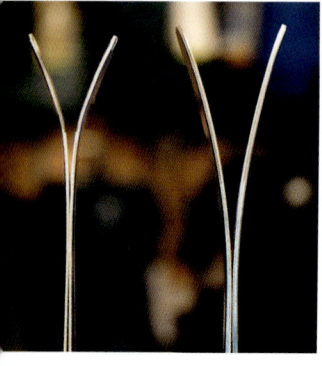

The ski on the right has more rocker than the ski on the left.

Skiers with a range of off-piste skis, all around head height.

Rocker

The rocker is the area that is not touching the surface when the ski is placed flat on the snow; the amount that it curls up at the front. A ski with more rocker will float through powder better but can feel less stable on firm snow as less base and edge are touching the snow. A ski with less rocker will grip better on firm snow, but not float as well in powder.

Length

Getting a ski which is around head height is a good general guide. If the ski has a large rocker, then you can have a longer ski, as less of the ski is actually in contact with the snow surface. If you are unsure between two lengths, ask for professional advice in a ski shop. Psychological factors can come into play here, so it is recommended to stand next to skis and see how you feel. If you are worried about them being too long, this is only going to be augmented when on the mountain.

PREPARATION

The skis on the right need waxing. The ski on the left has been freshly waxed.

Whichever skis you go for, ensure that they are serviced regularly, either at home or by a recommended ski technician. Remember, white bases equal dry bases. If the bases of your skis look white and feel dry, they need some wax.

Ski choice

Ski choice comes down to personal preference and is always going to be a compromise. For example, skis that are ideal for deep powder skiing in Japan will not be ideal for off-piste skiing in Scotland, where the snow is generally significantly less deep. Consider not only where you are going to be skiing but also who you will be skiing with. Someone on skis that are 120/90/110 with a 15m radius will ski the mountain in a very different way to someone with 130/120/125 with a 22m radius.

Ski servicing

Servicing skis regularly will result in a more effective performance, make skiing less tiring and more enjoyable, and prolong the life of the skis. For competition skiers, this is a lengthy and scientific process, which may be carried out by a dedicated team. However, for most off-piste skiers, this can be done by a specialist ski technician or at home, with a few tools and a basic understanding.

The general procedure is simplified here. When ski servicing, work from the tip to the tail of the ski, to go in the direction that the ski will travel in. It is best to place the skis in a vice.

Kit required for home servicing; waxing iron, base file, P-tex and lighter, metal scraper, edge file guide, edge file, diamond file, wax, plastic scraper and a brush.

OFF-PISTE PERFORMANCE

Bases
Wipe any dirt off the bases with cloth. Identify gouges which may need filling. Gouges that are through the first base material, or close to the edge of the ski, will need expert attention and are best repaired by a specialist ski technician. Smaller gouges can be filled by lighting a P-tex stick and dripping it onto the ski base. Let the P-tex set and then scrape it flat with a metal scraper.

If the base feels rough because of light scratches, smooth it using a base file.

Dripping P-tex into a small gouge (photo ▲).

Base filing the ski (photos ▶).

Edges
Skis will come from the factory with a specific edge angle on them, and this can normally be found on the relevant website. Most skis will have either a 90° or 88° edge angle. Set an edging tool to the desired edge angle and place the file firmly on the edge of the ski, with the guide on the base. Draw the file guide along the length of the ski. 88° edge is a more acute angle and therefore sharper and will grip better in firm conditions. 90° is fine for softer conditions. A disadvantage of choosing an 88° angle is that the edge becomes blunt faster. Once the edge is sharp use a diamond stone to polish the edges. Be cautious of edging skis too much as the edge is reduced every time they are filed. The edges can be particularly thin on lightweight skis. Using a diamond file is a good way to maintain the edges while minimising edge loss.

Sharpening the edges of the skis. Ensure the file is pulled (or pushed) in the correct direction (indicated by the arrow) so that small filings are removed from the edge. In the close-up (right-hand photo), the file is pulled from right to left.

PREPARATION

Wax

Wipe any filings off the ski with a dry cloth. Waxing is critical to the performance of your skis, making them slide more easily. Hot wax allows the wax to penetrate the base of the ski, lasting much longer than a rub-on wax. Selecting a suitable wax can be confusing, and a universal wax is a good one to choose if unsure. Generally, yellow waxes are for the warmest snow temperatures, red for cold snow temperatures, and blue and purple for very cold snow temperatures. Drip the wax over the base of the ski with an iron, then iron the wax until it is smooth. It is very important to keep the iron moving. Leave the wax to cool and then use a plastic scraper to remove the excess because it is the wax that is 'in' the base that is important. To finish, brush the base with a nylon or horsehair brush. The final brush should be in the direction of travel.

Waxing, scraping and brushing the ski.

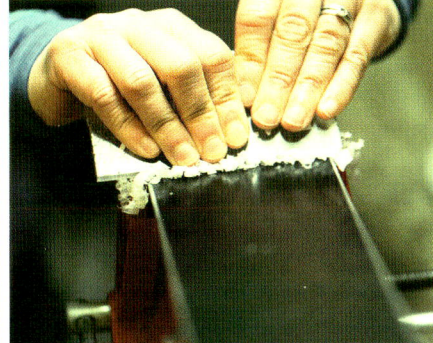

Ski Boots

Ski boots are a vital component in the connection between the body and the skis. Purchasing ski boots should be done via a specialist boot fitter who will spend time looking at your foot type and ask about what you will use the boot for. Alpine, hybrid and ski touring boots can all be used for skiing off-piste, the essential ingredient being that it is the right boot for your foot. A well-fitting pair of ski boots is crucial so that every movement that you make with your foot is directly transmitted to the ski. Avoid reading ski boot reviews in advance of visiting the boot fitter. It might be the highest-ranking ski boot in the reviews, but if it doesn't fit your foot then it may hinder performance rather than help it.

Ensure the chosen boot will work with your skis. For example, a lightweight ski touring boot is not designed to work with a wide, stiff ski. In this case, a better choice would be a heavier hybrid boot.

Lightweight ski touring boots tend to be thinner and therefore colder than a heavier weight boot. This can have implications for performance if you are intending to ski mostly from ski lifts. Warm feet are essential for enjoyment and being able to focus on the activity.

Alpine, hybrid and ski touring boots.

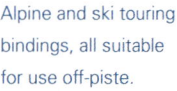 "I was in agony with my boots so I went to see a specialist boot fitter. He took one look at my socks and suggested this might be the problem. I returned to the hill the next day with new socks and the pain in my boots had vanished. This boot fitter was worth his weight in gold, giving me a simple solution to a significant problem. Invest in new socks regularly!"

Bindings

There is a vast array of bindings available. The priority is to ensure that your bindings are compatible with your chosen ski boots. This is best checked by a qualified ski technician, who can also set up your bindings. For instance, boots with the recently developed *GripWalk* soles (a new standard for alpine ski boots which is more comfortable, and grippier, for walking in) are no longer compatible with the old type of alpine bindings, because these need a smooth and hard front sole to release safely. Similarly, ski touring boots are generally not compatible with alpine bindings. Only boots with pin inserts in them will fit in a pin binding. Some boots come with interchangeable soles to allow usage in both alpine and touring bindings.

Ski touring and alpine bindings are both suitable for off-piste skiing. However, there is a significant advantage to having a ski touring binding (and skins), as it enables you to go back uphill to help someone if required, or reverse your route if needed. In firm snow conditions, walking up may be risky due to the potential consequences of a slip. In deep powder snow, uphill progress may be time-consuming, energy-sapping and sometimes, impossible. This is why it is strongly recommended to always carry skins (and consider ski crampons) when skiing off-piste, even if you have no planned intention of using them.

When selecting the best binding for off-piste skiing, consider what your primary use for the skis will be and what type of skier you are, then select

Alpine and ski touring bindings, all suitable for use off-piste.

This skier will certainly benefit from having skins if they need to ascend back uphill for any reason.

Walking on rocks and regular exposure to grit and salt can all have a detrimental impact on the workings of boots and bindings.

accordingly. Lightweight ski touring bindings are designed primarily for going uphill and heavier bindings are designed with downhill performance in mind. Hybrid freeride bindings are becoming increasingly common and offer a good compromise with strong downhill performance combined with the ability to skin uphill comfortably.

Ski brakes are recommended, especially if skiing within a resort, and they are mandatory in some areas. Ski mountaineering racers used to race without brakes to save weight, but in 2021 the International Ski Mountaineering Federation (ISMF) added brakes to the kit list for safety reasons. The benefit of brakes outweighs the gain from a small reduction in weight. The benefit is that the ski should stop if it releases, which avoids losing the ski, or worse, it flying off and hitting another skier. Leashes are an alternative option, but if the ski releases there are nasty consequences to falling with a ski attached to you, flapping around like a rotor blade.

Inspect both ski boots and bindings regularly for signs of wear which may affect the release mechanism.

DIN settings

Bindings must have the correct DIN setting range for you. DIN is an acronym derived from the German phrase 'Deutsches Institut für Normung', translated as the German Institute for Standardisation. This is an industry-wide scale of release force for ski bindings, on a scale of 0 to 24, with the upper ranges reserved for World Cup downhill racers and the majority of skiers using somewhere in the 4 – 12 range.

The DIN setting is designed to help reduce the risk of injury, by allowing the skis to release in the event of a fall. DIN setting is calculated by answering a series of questions relating to age, ability, sole length of boot, height and weight. There are apps available such as *dincalculator* that can be used to calculate your DIN value. Generally, heavier and more advanced skiers will require a higher DIN setting, while lighter and less experienced skiers will benefit from a lower DIN setting. This is not a grading system and the aim should not be to go up the DIN settings.

OFF-PISTE PERFORMANCE

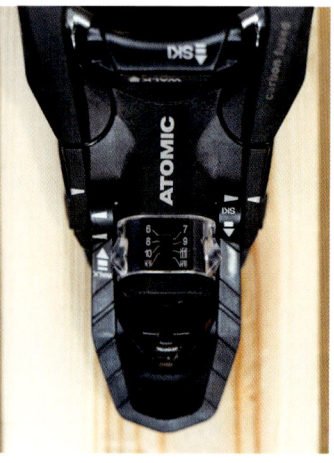

The DIN setting on the toe piece of the binding. This is set to 6, indicated by the white line.

Skier ❶ is not affected by ramp angle as the bindings are nearly flat. Skier ❷ has a significant ramp angle and is skiing in a similar position to skier ❶, but feels like they are too far forwards. Skier ❸ also has a significant ramp angle and in order to stay in balance near the centre of the skis, they have bent more from the knees, resulting in tired legs and sore knees.

The DIN setting should be calculated at the start of each season as the input variables will change with time. All of the input variables are objective, apart from the level of skier, which is subjective and can be confusing. For instance, you may have high technical ability, but prefer to ski at slow speeds on easy-angled terrain, does that mean you are intermediate or advanced? If unsure, input the variables with each suitable option and note down the different values. Normally there will only be a difference of 1, so a value between the two possibilities can be selected. DIN settings can be checked and adjusted at home or by a qualified ski technician.

Skiing injuries are often blamed on bindings not releasing during a fall. It's important to remember that if the fall hadn't happened, then the injury is far less likely to have occurred. While it is essential that bindings are correctly adjusted, the focus of attention then needs to shift to achieving optimum performance, hence avoiding falling wherever possible.

Ramp angle

Ramp angle describes the difference in height between the toe piece and the heel piece of the binding. On an alpine binding, this is normally relatively flat or close to zero. On touring bindings, the difference can be as great as 20mm. This is of greater significance for those with smaller feet, as the angle becomes steeper the closer the toe and heel pieces are together. Some skiers may perceive that this difference helps them to 'get forward', but in reality, those skiers tend to end up in the 'back seat' since their bodies naturally compensate for the additional forward tilt with additional knee bend and backwards lean. While this can work in certain situations, overall, it tends to cause poor control, tired muscles and knee strain. Ramp angle will also be affected by boots and insoles, but the greatest influence is from bindings. It can be adjusted by having plates fitted under the toe of the binding, bearing in mind that this will lift the skier further off the snow.

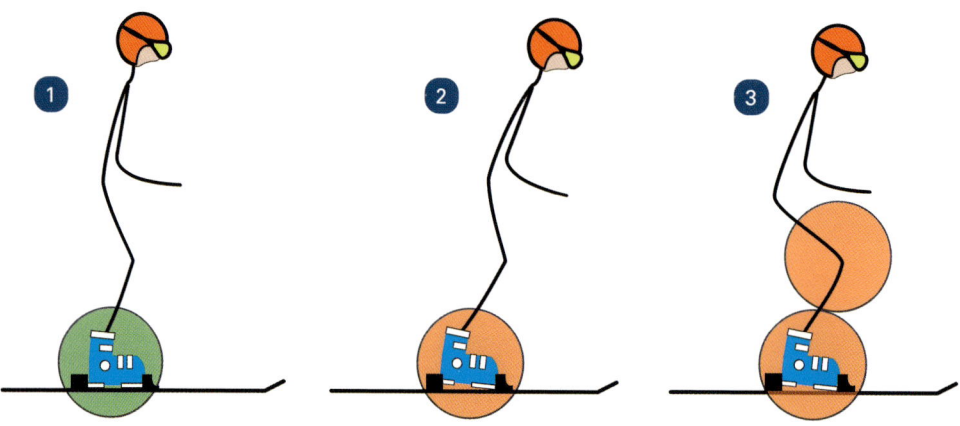

PREPARATION

The boot on the left has less ramp angle than the one on the right. While the difference looks subtle, it is significant.

The crucial thing to remember is that the balance point will be affected by ramp angle, and in turn, it will influence performance. Ultimately, it comes down to personal preference.

💡 "For years, whenever I went ski touring, I felt like I was skiing wearing high heels, and I got very tired legs and sore knees. I put it down to poor fitness and technique, although I was puzzled why I didn't feel the same when skiing off-piste on my alpine kit. Then I was introduced to the concept of ramp angle, and new bindings revolutionised my off-piste skiing. I have size EU 36 feet. Now, low ramp angle is my major deciding factor when buying ski touring bindings."

Measuring ski poles to check they are the correct length.

Ski poles

To find the correct length of pole, stand on flat ground with ski boots on, turn the pole upside down and hold it just under the basket. The pole is the correct length if the angle of the elbow is approximately a right angle.

This is only a guide as there are situations where longer or shorter poles may be preferable. Longer poles can be better for steeper slopes so that balance and support can be gained from the pole. In contrast, mogul skiers use shorter poles as they encourage more flex and lateral movement.

Adjustable poles are a good idea as the length can be changed for different situations. However, this is another link that can be prone to breaking. A good solution is a pole with a lengthy grip so that the hand position can be changed for different situations.

Long grips on ski poles.

 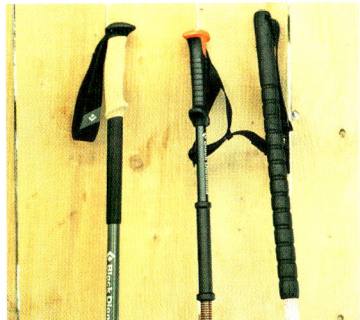

35

OFF-PISTE PERFORMANCE

The larger basket on the left is most suitable for off-piste skiing.

Ski poles should have large baskets on the bottom to prevent them from sinking too deep into powder snow.

Most poles will come with straps on them. Skiers may choose to remove these completely for skiing off-piste but some skiers find that this can lead to a loss of positivity with the pole plant. It is advisable to ski with hands out of the straps in trees or vegetation, in case the basket of your pole gets stuck in the undergrowth.

Helmet

A well-fitting and comfortable helmet, certified for skiing, is strongly recommended. Some helmets are certified for both skiing (EN1077) and climbing (EN12492), which is worth considering if you plan to combine those activities and particularly if going ski touring. Select a helmet that fits your head, is comfortable, and does not overly restrict vision or hearing. You've got to like it to wear it! Try on helmets with goggles to ensure they are a good fit.

Goggles

Goggles are recommended when skiing as they give far greater eye protection than sunglasses in the event of a fall. While this can be challenging in bright conditions, Category 4 goggles are available, which are ideal for sunny spring conditions.

If it's at all damp then carry two pairs of goggles. Once the foam gets wet, the goggles will steam up and this is very difficult to rectify while out

A range of certified ski helmets.

Goggles with changeable lenses for different light conditions.

PREPARATION

on the hill. Avoid putting your goggles on top of a wet helmet for this reason: once they are on your face, keep them on your face.

Different colours of lenses are available for different light conditions, but what works for one person may not work for another as our eyes are all different. If you are looking for a flat light lens, go shopping on a flat light day, step outside the shop and look at the snow to find what works best for you.

Rucksack

Look for a ski-specific rucksack with a ski-carrying system and a dedicated, easily accessible place to store rescue equipment. Try it on with all of your belongings inside to see how stable it is on your back. Then do some ski movements such as jumping up and down and see how much the rucksack moves around. You are aiming for a rucksack that moves as part of your body, rather than moving independently.

A selection of off-piste skiing rucksacks (photo ▶).

Rucksack with a dedicated, easily accessible pocket for shovel and probe (photo far ▶).

Transceiver, shovel and probe.

Transceiver, shovel and probe

A transceiver, shovel and probe are essential when skiing outside of patrolled ski runs; anywhere off-piste. In some countries this has become mandatory. It is important to be familiar and well-practised with your own kit.

OFF-PISTE PERFORMANCE

Skiers that are alert and ready for learning, keeping warm by wearing suitable clothing that isn't restricting movement.

Clothing

Temperature regulation can be challenging when doing sport in the winter environment, constantly varying between times of standing around in the cold or being on lifts, to high-energy bursts of exercise which quickly warm the body. Nevertheless, effective temperature regulation is important for optimum performance. It's a balancing act to keep the body warm enough to be alert and ready to take on new learning, but unrestricted in movement by having too many clothes. Aim to have a suitable layering system that allows for layers to be added and removed as required, and ensure that movements are free and unhindered by the clothing.

ENVIRONMENT

In off-piste skiing there are many environmental factors which are constantly changing and will influence performance, such as snow type, terrain, weather and altitude. These variations are often a big attraction of off-piste skiing but also present many challenges. The challenges of varying terrain and snow types are addressed later in the book.

In Scotland for many years now, you have to be opportunistic to make the most of the conditions. This is making the most of a rare blue bird powder day. A few days later most of the snow in the photo had disappeared.

"I skied off-piste for many years rarely finding good snow. In January, I was always too late in the day, with the powder already tracked out or having turned to gloop after a rise in temperature. In April, I was always too early, often skiing on horrible refrozen snow. As a result, rarely did I enjoy off-piste skiing and there was limited motivation to improve. Often it was a case of just surviving, rather than being in a place where I could purposely practise. Through experience and observations, and going on a few courses, I learned to find the good snow, the stuff that was fun to ski. I enjoyed it, I did more and I found opportunities to relax and practise new techniques. As a result, my performance came on in leaps and bounds, all because I learned how to find good snow."

Changing conditions

It is undeniable that snow reliability through the winter is cause for concern due to the effects of climate change. Conditions are less predictable and extreme weather events are becoming more common. This increases the need for versatility in our off-piste ski technique. In order to maximise our time on skis, we need to seek enjoyment from a wider spectrum of off-piste conditions, relishing the challenge of every condition that off-piste skiing can deliver, not just waiting for the powder days. "I'll wait till later in the season" or "I'll come next season" are commonly heard phrases, but it does not mean anything better is coming. We should make the most of the snow when we have it. The more snow types and terrain features we find enjoyable, the more we can keep enjoying skiing as the winters become progressively less predictable. Being efficient at turning in small spaces is key to getting enjoyment from a thin strip of snow. Linking patches of snow together can be fun and feel creative. We need to be on top form physically and mentally, being opportunistic when our favourite snow types arrive, and still enjoy striving to make the perfect turn even when the conditions aren't perfect.

"I was working with a group of top-level instructors on an off-piste mountain safety exam. We had skinned for over 1,200m to reach a north facing bowl that held a short pitch of beautifully soft untracked powder, which had been so rare this season. We were all very excited and rushed to ski the pitch. After twenty turns or so we regrouped at the bottom, everyone slightly deflated by our sub-optimal performances, myself included. We are high-level performers, why had this happened? We took some time to reflect on why our descents had not felt as fluid as we had all expected. It had been a lean season and none of us had skied powder for over six weeks, only firm hard-packed snow. We hadn't been ready psychologically, technically, or tactically to make the most of this pitch of powder, which had been over all too soon. In hindsight, we should have taken a moment at the top to focus on the conditions, the change in snow type and plan how we would need to adjust our movements and balance. During most seasons these adjustments would be instinctive from skiing powder regularly. My learning point from this day was always to take a moment to tune in to the conditions. Simply visualising myself skiing in the conditions ahead helps me to achieve optimal performance."

WARM UP

Warming up is normally used in reference to the physical components, however, it is of great benefit to have a warm-up routine, however basic and simple, across all of the performance components, starting the evening before the activity. Think of a warm-up as a preparation routine.

- Watch the weather forecast the night before skiing (environment). Think of the implication this has on your kit selection (equipment), choice of route and the influences this will have on the snow (environment). Will you be skiing spring snow or powder?
- Prepare kit. Lay out appropriate kit for the day's skiing. This may include waxing skis (equipment). Which wax will be required given the current snow temperature (environment)?
- Have a suitable meal and stay hydrated (physical).
- Visualise the nature of tomorrow's skiing (psychological).
- Get a good night's sleep (physical).
- Have a suitable breakfast (physical).
- Journey to the ski area and make observations about the weather. How much snow has fallen overnight? Is the snow melting off the car and the trees (environment)? This journey may involve some walking (physical).
- Traversing through the off-piste snow to get a feel for the snow conditions (physical, psychological, environment, tactical and technical).

Off-piste skiers ready to ski after a preparation routine that began the night before.

On the opposite page are a few warm-up exercises which can be done before setting off downhill.

Any of the drills later in the book which are done without skis on, are also great warm-up exercises.

💡 "I often found myself complaining that there wasn't time to warm up when off-piste skiing, like there can be when skiing on the piste. The first turns could be challenging, sometimes starting from a mountain hut where we had stayed overnight. Rarely did I ski well first thing in the morning. More recently I have adopted an all-encompassing approach, viewing the warm-up as much broader than just a physical one. Where there is less opportunity to warm up physically, I place greater emphasis on the other components, for example using more mental rehearsal. If the first turns look challenging, I warm up by rehearsing some skiing movements without travelling on the skis. I can also traverse through the snow initially to get used to the prevailing environmental conditions. With this approach, I find that I can ski much better first thing in the morning and get more enjoyment from the whole day."

Moving the leg back and forwards to loosen up the hip joint (photo ▲).
Rotating the leg within the hip socket to warm up the joint laterally (photo ◀).
Ask a partner to hold a ski pole vertically. Stand about two metres back. The partner should drop the pole without warning, giving no indication as to which way it will fall. Try to catch the pole before it touches the ground. This will warm up the mind and body, ready for making quick adjustments (photos ▼).

PRACTICE ON THE HILL

All too often skiers train physically for skiing before they ski, but once on the hill, they just go skiing. Skiing mileage is important, but it is also essential that time is spent 'training' once on the mountain to achieve optimum performance.

Training ground

In golf, there are driving ranges, in climbing, there are bouldering walls, in mountain biking, there are skills parks, all of which are used as training grounds. For off-piste skiing, the training ground is the piste. The piste can be used for drills and focused practice, much more than just a pathway for getting from one section of off-piste to another.

Time on skis

Try to calculate how much time you spend skiing. During one day of skiing, how much time is actually spent moving on skis? When time is deducted for lifts, rests, decision-making, and chatting, the moving time is much lower than expected. During a full day of skiing, the actual moving time is unlikely to exceed two hours. How much of this time is intensive practice? If you skied fifty days a year, this is 100 hours of skiing a year. Anders Ericsson's research developed the idea that 10,000 hours of practice is required to achieve mastery of complex skills. Although this figure is debatable and there are varying opinions of its validity, with fifty days of skiing a year, this would take one hundred years to reach!

When ski touring, the time spent skiing downhill is far less than when skiing off the lifts. On an average off-piste day skiing from the lifts, a skier might typically cover between 5,000 and 10,000 metres of descent. This is similar to the descent that would be covered in a week's ski touring trip.

We shouldn't be disheartened by this knowledge, but rather use it to ensure that every moment on skis is time well spent, aiming for quality purposeful practice time. Visualising ski performance is a great way to up the hours of practice if the time on snow is limited. Rumour has it that the legendary Italian slalom skier Alberto Tomba, following an intensive day of training on the hill, completed an additional twenty runs in the evening, all in his head!

Repetition

Pick only one aspect to focus on at a time, and think of this element for a few runs, aiming to minimise other distractions. Saying a word that relates to what you are working on out loud will help to stay focused on that element. Three runs in the same place, maximum four, is good for practice, then change the area used to adapt your skills to a different environment. For example, if working on moving forward into the turn (from Key Movements), say 'hip' out loud as you initiate each turn, as a trigger word to remind you to move forward. Once you become comfortable with doing this movement in one place, do the same in another place, as the conditions will undoubtedly be different.

Physical training on skis

Spend time training the physical aspect on skis, as well as the technical aspects, by varying the length of pitch skied and operating in different gears, not just one. For example, do some interval training on skis, where you work really hard for a short pitch, say fifteen turns, stop and rest for one minute and then repeat. Then pick a lower gear and try to do a run non-stop.

ESSENTIAL SKILLS

Descending the Argentière Glacier in Chamonix, an off-piste journey which can involve all of these essential skills.

There are a number of technical skills which are essential when skiing off-piste. These skills are very similar to the essential skills needed on-piste but need to be well-practised, ready to be deployed effectively in any situation, whatever the weather and snow conditions. For example, putting skis on in deep snow, on a steep slope, in windy conditions is considerably more challenging than doing it outside a café, on flat terrain with compacted snow.

STATIC SKILLS

These skills occur on the spot, as opposed to when travelling down the slope. Therefore, they can easily be practised in a quiet area away from other people and they can be rehearsed away from snow. For example, if you struggle getting up from a fall, time spent practising on a grassy slope will be beneficial, before adding in the additional complication of skis sinking into soft snow. Similarly, if you are using pin bindings for the first time, practising stepping into them away off the snow where there is no risk of the skis sliding off down the slope.

Putting skis on

Make this your preferred method of putting skis on in all situations, then it will become ingrained and habitual, so there is less risk of getting it wrong when on steeper terrain. A ski sliding off down the hill can be dangerous both on and off-piste, and this method helps to prevent that happening. This method presumes there is no use of an ice axe, which mountaineers may have with them, to help create a flat platform.

Start by selecting the flattest area that you can. If there is no flat ground, create a flat platform that is perpendicular to the slope. This can be done by either kicking into the snow with your boots or using the ski to create a level platform. If a platform can't be created due to the firmness of the snow, assistance can be gained from a partner by having them place a pole underneath the ski to create a platform. Watch out for trapped fingers! Don't forget that when skiing off-piste, you'll have a shovel in your rucksack, which can be used for creating a platform too.

Next, clear any snow off the bottom of your boots to ensure an accurate location of the boot into the binding. This can be done by banging one boot

Placing a pole underneath the ski to create a flat platform, when putting skis on.

The snow must be removed from the base of the boot before clicking into the binding.

against the other boot, but care needs to be taken so as not to damage the buckles. Alternatively, the boot can be scraped over the binding, but again this needs to be done carefully to avoid damaging the front of the binding. Often the best way is to ask a partner to scrape the snow off with the end of their ski pole or a scraper (a useful item to carry).

Always put the bottom ski on first. This is the hardest ski to put on, so this is a system that gives the greatest stability when clipping into the bottom ski.

1. Stand beneath the skis, with skis and feet perpendicular to the fall line, facing in the direction that you wish to set off in.
2. If the snow allows, insert the tails of the skis into the snow to stop them from sliding away.
3. Insert ski poles, upside down, into the snow, to be used for increased stability (this may not be possible in firm snow).
4. Cross the downhill foot, in front and above, the uphill foot, to click into the binding of the ski that is on the downhill side of the platform. Use poles for stability.
5. Move the remaining foot around to click into the other binding. Remove poles from the snow, ready to ski.

Crossing the downhill foot, in front and above, the uphill foot (photos ▼ ▶).

Clicking into the second binding (photo ▶).

OFF-PISTE PERFORMANCE

The skier has created a flat platform, for putting skis on or taking them off.

Taking skis off
This reverses the process of putting skis on.
1. Create a flat platform, perpendicular to the slope.
2. Insert ski poles, upside down, into the slope for increased stability.
3. Release the uphill foot and step out of the binding.
4. Put the removed ski vertically into the snow to avoid it sliding off (this may not be possible in firm snow).
5. Place this foot beneath the remaining horizontal ski, so that it is in a position to support the ski should it start to slide.
6. Remove the downhill ski and place it vertically into the snow.

Removing skis in off-piste terrain.

ESSENTIAL SKILLS

Fall line

The fall line in skiing is an imaginary line which runs directly downhill from the skier. For example, it is the line which a ball would take if you rolled it downhill, under the influence of gravity. On a map, the fall line is perpendicular to the contour lines. It's helpful to be aware of the fall line as you will use it as a reference for the actions that you need to make with your skis. For example, you may be given the instruction 'turn your skis until they are perpendicular to the fall line' and to be able to do this, you will need to understand where the fall line is.

The majority of pistes follow the fall line, although sometimes the piste will cross the fall line to avoid hazards or to take the skiers to a specific point on the mountain. This can result in an uneven feeling to your skiing, with the turn in one direction feeling completely different to the other.

Similarly, when skiing off-piste, the most desired line is the fall line but skiers sometimes need to go across the fall line to avoid a hazard, find the best snow, or get to a specific point on the mountain.

The fall line is highlighted by the arrows.

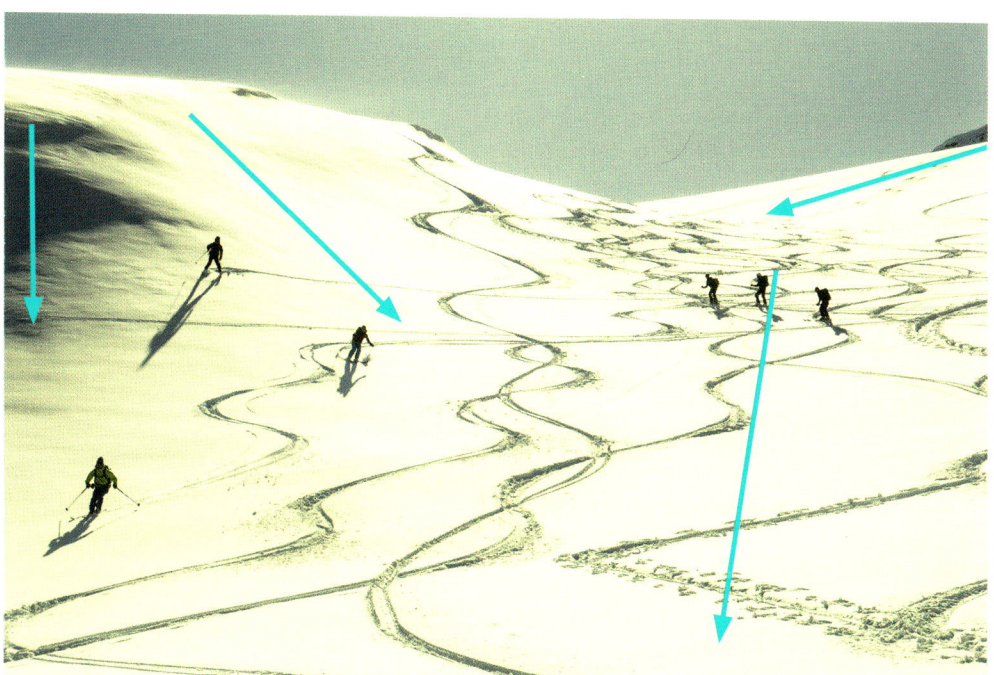

OFF-PISTE PERFORMANCE

Ski poles in a cross on the uphill side to create a platform that doesn't sink into the snow.

Getting up from a fall

1. From whatever tangled position you find yourself in, work around until the skis are beneath you, and perpendicular to the fall line. This is essential, otherwise, as you start to get up you will find the skis run forwards or backwards.
2. Place the ski poles in a cross on your uphill side to create a platform that doesn't sink into the snow. This is particularly useful in deep snow.
3. Push down on the crossed poles with your hand. At the same time, roll your head forwards and down towards the snow and push your bottom up into the air. Uncurl as you come up, with your head coming up last.

The process of getting up from a fall. Think of bottom up first, head up last.

ESSENTIAL SKILLS

Take your rucksack off and place it underneath your hip, to reduce the weight on your back and to create an artificial slope, both making it considerably easier to get up.

If you are struggling to get up, take your rucksack off and place it under your hip. This has two benefits. It takes the weight off your back and also provides an artificial slope so that your body is at an angle. This can be particularly helpful on flat ground.

It can also help to take off the uphill ski. Do this once you have got yourself into a position perpendicular to the slope. This will mean that you are able to adjust the position of the uphill foot to a place where you are more able to push up on it.

While it's very important to practise getting up on your own, if someone is there offering a hand then take it, as it will conserve energy.

It can help to take the uphill ski off.

49

OFF-PISTE PERFORMANCE

Sit down turn

You may find yourself in a situation where you need to turn and you can't. For example, you may be faced with breakable crust at the end of a long day and your legs are tired. Ideally, you would avoid turning by using a descending traverse, but you may need to turn if you run out of snow or there is an obstacle. A sit down turn isn't graceful, but it's good to know that it's allowed! Sit down, flip the skis over, and stand up again. This sounds simple but it does require a degree of flexibility, so it is recommended to practise this skill before it is required and to practise in the company of others in case you get stuck.

The skier has run out of options so decides to sit down, flip their skis over and then stand up again.

In a situation where, for whatever reason, you would rather avoid turning, one course of action may be to take the skis off and walk. However, this can be dangerous and should be avoided in the majority of circumstances due to:
- Being on an icy or firm slope where the risk of falling, and sliding, will increase without skis on.
- Being on a glacier where the risk of falling in a crevasse is elevated without skis on.
- Being in deep snow where any progress, uphill or downhill, can be both time-consuming and energy-sapping.

MOVEMENT SKILLS

This section covers skills that are essential for manoeuvring around the mountainside when 'skiing' the slope is not appropriate. This may be due to the gradient, snow type, or obstacles such as rocks or trees. These skills can also be incorporated into any descent, at any time, to give a flowing run, often acting as a key link between turns. Watch a freeride competition and you'll see plenty of positive, and fast, side slipping and traversing between the turns.

A good off-piste skier will deploy these skills when they recognise a psychological barrier to executing a good turn. If there is a feeling of intimidation about the turn, and there is a significant consequence to getting it wrong, it's far better to play it safe and use one of these skills. All of these skills should be practised regularly so that they can be adopted as a positive tactic in challenging situations.

The skier is side slipping until they are confident that they can perform the turn with a high level of accuracy, as they are in a place where there is little margin for error.

> "I found myself skiing in a group where others were happy to turn in places that I wasn't. I realised that I had to refine my techniques for moving around the mountain when I didn't want to 'ski' the slope or had to negotiate technical sections. Therefore, as an off-piste skier, I regularly spend time refining the skills that I first learned as a beginner skier; working on my side stepping, side slipping, traversing and snowploughing. I now find that I can keep up with my group as I continue to make progress down the mountain, even though I may not wish to turn."

OFF-PISTE PERFORMANCE

Side stepping

Side stepping is the action of stepping down the slope, accurately placing one ski at a time, while the skis remain perpendicular to the fall line. Side stepping can also be used for ascending a short section.

Throughout this process, the body should be aligned as when standing, with the head over the feet. A common mistake is for the upper body to tilt forward, resulting in the skis sliding backwards. Avoid this by looking ahead rather than down, or glancing down at the skis by flexing at the neck, not the waist.

For descending, the downhill ski should be lifted a short distance downhill, far enough to make downhill progress but close enough to maintain balance and so that the lower leg is still flexed. The ski should be placed accurately, perpendicular to the slope. The uphill ski should then be moved in

Skier side stepping through a rocky section, glancing down, flexing from the neck, with the body aligned over the feet, making accurate foot placements and having a good stabilising pole position.

ESSENTIAL SKILLS

line with the downhill ski, and the process repeated to make progress down the slope. If either ski slides forwards or backwards, this is an indication that the skis are not perpendicular to the slope and an adjustment needs to be made. If the ski slides forwards, the tip of the ski needs to be adjusted to point further uphill. If the ski slides backwards, the tip of the ski needs to be adjusted to point further downhill.

Throughout this manoeuvre, the poles should be positioned in line with the front binding and used to aid stability, but not pressed down upon.

Step by Feel

Try side stepping on a piste without looking at the skis, and aim for no movement of the skis when they are on the snow, maintaining complete control throughout the process. This will help to maintain a good body position and gain a good feel for where the skis are in relation to the fall line.

The skier is side stepping without looking down at the skis, to help maintain a good body position.

Side slipping

Side slipping is a continuation of side stepping, but the skis remain on the snow. Both skis are slid down the hill in unison, rather than placed one at a time. It should be a positive and decisive action to lose height without traversing, with a high level of accuracy for the direction of travel, not only straight down the hill but also forwards and backwards.

OFF-PISTE PERFORMANCE

Gradually release the edges of the skis so the skis become flatter. Let the skis drift sideways down the hill while they remain perpendicular to the slope. Re-engage the edges to slow down or stop, and feel the skis grip. If you find yourself drifting forwards, then the tips of the skis need to be turned further up the hill. If you find yourself drifting backwards, the tips need to be turned further down the hill. These adjustments are subtle but significant.

Side slipping can be done successfully with the upper body in line with the skis, or with the upper body facing down the hill. In both situations, the upper body is quiet and detached from the action of the skis.

Side slipping, showing the release and re-engagement of the edges of the ski.

Side slipping is often used as an integral part of skiing to link one turn to the next, giving a good way to control speed and line. It is a useful tool to maintain flow and movement, rather than stopping and then having to start from stationary.

Side slipping can be preferable to side stepping in narrow places such as couloirs as it smooths the slope rather than puts steps in it, making it more favourable for others that follow behind. However, in thin snow conditions, it may be better to side step, as sliding may remove all the snow to leave ice or rock for those that follow.

Skier side slipping accurately with the upper body facing down the hill.

ESSENTIAL SKILLS

Skiers side slipping accurately with the upper body facing across the hill. In the second photo, the performance could be improved if the skier looked in their direction of travel.

Both side stepping and side slipping are good for developing edge awareness and control, which will benefit many other aspects of off-piste skiing, such as control on icy slopes, skiing in bumps, and the ability to do turns in small spaces.

 **Slide on a Line**

Imagine, or ask a friend to draw, a line running down the hill, firstly running straight down the fall line, then deviating backwards and forwards. Try to follow it in a side slip, with your feet staying on the line. Remember, if you feel that you go forwards off the line, adjust your skis so that the tips of the skis are slightly further up the hill and the tails are slightly further down the hill. If you go backwards from the line, let the tips of your skis come slightly further down the hill, and the tails of your skis come slightly further up the hill.

Side slipping while aiming to stay within the poles and not touch them.

This can also be done by placing poles to create a corridor for the skier to stay within.

Races

Side slipping (or side stepping) races can be a great way to improve speed, accuracy, and confidence. This helps the skill become a positive, decisive action, rather than a defensive one.

Snowploughing

Skiers normally learn how to snowplough in their first few days, if not hours, on skis, and the skill should always remain part of the skier's toolbox, particularly when it comes to off-piste skiing. A snowplough does exactly what it says, it ploughs snow out of the way, which is often required off-piste. The term 'stem' is sometimes used, and this generally refers to when the outside ski is lifted and 'placed' in a triangle shape, as opposed to a snowplough where the ski remains on the snow. The concept and application are the same for off-piste skiing. It is making a triangle shape with the skis, which puts the uphill ski on its new edge, ensuring that it is in a good position to plough snow out of the way. Conversely, a ski that is flat against the surface of the snow cannot push any snow out of the way.

Edged skis can push snow out of the way. Notice the build-up of snow around the boots as it is pushed out of the way (photo ▶).

A flat ski in snow, unable to push snow out of the way, hence the ski will feel 'trapped' (photo ▲).

> "As a basic parallel skier, I kept falling over when I tried to ski off-piste, determined not to let my technique regress to snowplough. Then I had a complete shift of mindset and started using my snowplough to initiate the turn, and my progress was immense. I felt like I had created a platform to push snow out of the way, rather than trying to turn in it. I found turning much easier and was no longer falling over. I had much greater control over where I was going, and soon the small triangle shape was barely visible."

Time spent practising and refining, or even just re-familiarising yourself with the action, will pay dividends later, particularly when it comes to skiing in challenging snow types, like breakable crust and heavy powder. A snowplough should be a positive action, used with confidence and assertiveness.

ESSENTIAL SKILLS

Snowploughing

Using a small snowplough to initiate the turn, so that snow can easily be pushed out of the way.

Go back to basics and practise some snowplough turns. Then decrease the size of the snowplough, but still have a small triangle to get the benefit of having one ski on its new edge before the turn, ready to plough the snow out of the way.

A deliberate snowplough, used with confidence and assertiveness.

OFF-PISTE PERFORMANCE

Traversing

This is the motion of travelling across the hill, rather than down it. The concept sounds simple but it is often not practised when skiing around pistes, which generally follow the fall line and rarely go sideways.

Historically, skiers were taught to traverse with their upper bodies facing down the mountain. With advances in ski technology and biomechanical understanding, this idea has changed. The upper body should face where the momentum is going; across the hill. This means you are in a strong and balanced position to be able to absorb any undulations on the traverse.

In order to control speed while traversing, the skier needs space to pivot the tips of the skis uphill, and the tails of the skis down the hill. Often, there is an 'edge' to a traversing line, which the skier might actively try to avoid for fear of falling off it. However, putting your feet on the edge opens up space to pivot the tips and tails of the skis, making it easier to control speed.

Traversing with both legs flexed equally, the upper body following the line of momentum (photo ▼).

The tracks show where skiers have traversed to find the safest line and best snow (photo ◤).

> "I had spent years clinging to the uphill side of a traversing line, staying as far away from the edge as I could. I found I would get faster and faster as I went across, with no way to control my speed. I was doubtful of placing my feet close to the 'edge' that I had so desperately been trying to avoid falling off. But by doing so, I could control my skis much better and as a result, I was no longer fearful of going over the edge."

Traversing is frequently linked with side slipping, making it possible to descend the whole mountain without turning or to manoeuvre effectively and efficiently to somewhere good to turn.

Another time when all of these essential skills may be called upon is if faced with a need to get off the mountain in a challenging situation, for example, if there has been an equipment failure or an injury.

ESSENTIAL SKILLS

The skier has deliberately placed their feet on the edge of the traversing line. This leaves the tips and the tails free and easy to pivot to control speed.

"I became incredibly grateful for my ability to traverse and side slip when I had a binding failure at the top of a mountain in a remote place where rescue would have been complex. I was able to strap the ski to my foot to make it secure, but I didn't want to exert any extra force on it by turning. I traversed and side slipped 1,000m, with the occasional sit down turn when I wanted to change direction, to make it safely off the mountain!"

KEY MOVEMENTS

Skiing off-piste terrain that requires a blend of all three key movements (photos ▲ ◀).

At first glance, off-piste technique can seem like a complex subject, and the intricacies of the detail can be overwhelming and confusing. However, by focusing on simple concepts it becomes easier to understand, practise and ultimately achieve optimum performance. To ski proficiently off-piste we need to be good at balancing, as this puts us in an effective position to turn the skis. When out of balance, turning the skis can feel like a battle. When in balance, turning the skis can feel effortless.

There are three different key movements that aid balance, and there are two distinct ways in which we can turn our skis.

Off-piste technique – A simple concept. We need to be good at balancing, to be in an effective position to turn our skis.

The same movements and ways of turning apply for beginner and intermediate skiers, as they do for World Cup skiers, ski instructors and guides, and free-ride professionals. This chapter looks at the three key movements to aid balance and the following chapter focuses on the two different ways of turning.

Each of the key movements is transferable from piste skiing. After all, both piste and off-piste are about travelling efficiently on snow. Time spent practising and refining these key movements on-piste will be hugely beneficial to off-piste skiing. When practising, it is important to understand how these movements link to off-piste skiing to motivate the practice.

OFF-PISTE PERFORMANCE

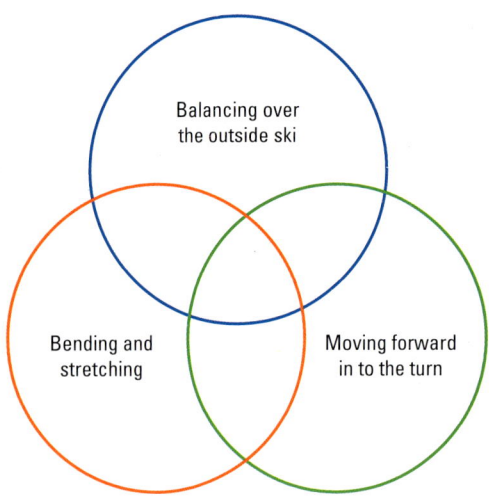

The three key movements of 1) balancing over the outside ski, 2) bending and stretching and 3) moving forward into the turn, are all closely intertwined.

These movements will need to be revisited time and time again as progress is made and practised in all different snow types and on varying terrain. The dynamic environment of skiing off-piste means that constant changes are necessary, but these changes are often simply small variations of these key movements. The movements are described here in isolation for simplicity, understanding, and ease of practice. However, in most performances they become closely intertwined, with the rate and range of each movement being variable, leading to infinite possible outcomes.

Focus on one movement at a time, both when reading and practising. Often when striving to improve performance, it is a case of one movement is missing, or needing development or exaggeration. With practice, you will be able to understand and feel which movement needs to be worked on to improve performance, which will vary from day to day, run to run, or even from turn to turn.

BALANCING OVER THE OUTSIDE SKI

It is essential to be able to balance over the outside ski throughout the whole turn. We don't always need to balance on the outside ski, but it's essential to have the ability to do so when required. This is a movement, not a static position. If doing continuous turns, then continuous movement is needed to stay in balance over the outside ski, as the outside ski changes from turn to turn.

What is balancing over the outside ski?

The key word to focus on is 'balancing'. This isn't pressing, or pushing, it is simply balancing. When done successfully it will feel like you could lift the inside ski off the snow if you wanted to. The transition from balancing on one ski to the other comes when the skis are perpendicular, or close to perpendicular, to the fall line.

These off-piste skiers, all performing at different levels, are well balanced over the outside ski.

KEY MOVEMENTS

 Inside or outside, lower or upper?

Skiers can be confused by which is the inside ski and which is the outside ski, this can be further complicated by references to the lower ski and upper ski. Think of the turn as two parallel semi-circular lines in the snow, one inside the other. The outside line (the longer line) is the path of the outside ski and the inside line (shorter line) is the path of the inside ski. Notice that the upper ski is the outside ski at the start of the turn, and the lower ski is the outside ski at the end of the turn. Try walking around a turn without skis on to get a feel for which is the outside ski. This can even be done in the comfort of your own home and visualised using your hands to replicate the action of the outside and inside skis.

Throughout the book, the terminology used will primarily be the outside and inside ski, unless referring to a traversing situation where lower and upper ski may be used.

Refer to this diagram for clarification of later mentions of the outside and inside ski. The outside ski is indicated by the red lines and the inside ski by the blue lines.

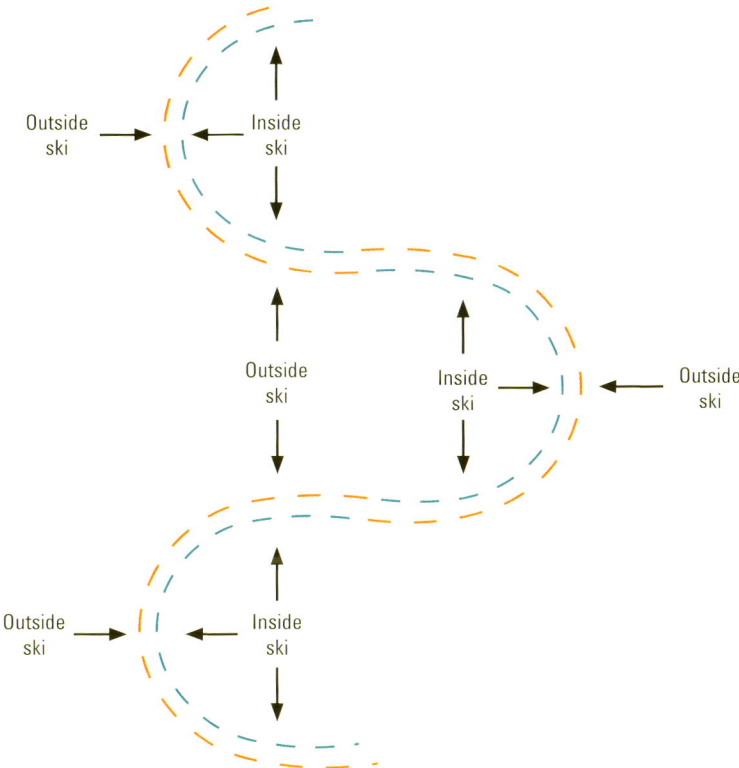

OFF-PISTE PERFORMANCE

Why is this required off-piste?
When deviating away from the fall line, balancing over the outside ski is fundamental in all skiing. You can get away without doing this on-piste and still move successfully around the mountain. This changes dramatically when skiing off-piste. Balancing over the outside ski is essential to maintain control through ever-changing terrain and snow types.

Imagine travelling in a straight line down the hill. To maintain good balance the skier will balance equally over both skis. As soon as you deviate from this line the balance over the outside ski needs to be increased, otherwise you may fall into the mountain.

These skiers have all lost balance over their outside ski coming out of the turn and are now balancing primarily on their inside ski. They are feeling, or about to feel, their uphill hand touching the snow, which in some cases resulted in a fall. You'll see freeriders, world-cup skiers and instructors all losing balance over the outside ski. It's happened to everyone!

The further you deviate from the fall line, the more you need to balance over the outside ski.

Balancing over the outside ski allows the inside ski to be free and not blocked. It will then be able to match the movements of the outside ski, so both skis will be able to work together. As skiers become better at balancing over the outside ski, they will be able to use the mountain more to help to control their speed.

Skiers who aren't skilful at balancing over the outside ski tend to ski a straighter line and don't come perpendicular to the fall line, since they don't feel stable in this position. This then results in the skier getting faster and faster,

Balancing equally over both skis when coming straight down the fall line (photo ▶).

Starting to deviate from the fall line, being well balanced over the outside ski (photo far ▶).

KEY MOVEMENTS

as they can't use the mountain effectively to control their speed. Not being balanced over the outside ski can also cause the skis to accelerate and shoot across the hill, feeling like your weight is back and that you are no longer able to control the skis. In this case, feeling like your weight is back is the symptom not the cause. The cause is not being well balanced over the outside ski.

How to do it well

In order to balance over the outside ski effectively, the upper body needs to move to stay over the outside foot (or ski). Rather than the body being in a straight line, the body separates in the middle, to create a curve or a 'C' shape. Some people find it helpful to think of this as a banana shape, or as a 'side to side' movement, going from one "C" to another "C". Throughout this book it is referred to as 'C' shape, as this roughly represents the shape the body will create. The body will be in a curve rather than a straight line, so "C" also stands for curve. When done correctly, you will feel a stretch on one side of the body and a squeeze on the other. This is technically known as lateral separation as the upper body has separated laterally from the lower body.

These skiers have no lateral separation, as indicated by the line through their bodies, and are not well balanced over the outside ski. A fall may be imminent (photos ▼◢)!

These skiers have separated their legs and upper body laterally and are well balanced over the outside ski, showing a 'C' curve shape (photos ▶◢).

OFF-PISTE PERFORMANCE

Hand on Knee

A simple way to help balance over the outside ski is to put a hand on the side of the outside knee through the whole turn. This helps to get a feeling of the movement with the body and the transition point. By placing the hand on the knee, the balance point automatically moves over the outside ski as the hand reaching down encourages the body into a 'C' shape. Ensure that the hand is placed on the side of the knee by bending the body sideways, not forwards.

Hand on Knee drill, helping to develop 'C' shape and therefore better balance over the outside ski.

KEY MOVEMENTS

Aeroplane Arms

This is a very similar drill to Hand on Knee. This drill helps to exaggerate the movement further, helps with the timing of the movement, and gives a clear indication of the transition from one side to the other. You'll often see children doing this in a ski school line, with one child at the back doing it the wrong way and getting little benefit from the drill! Put the outside hand down towards the outside foot and the inside arm high. Smoothly change from one side to the other when the skis are perpendicular to the fall line.

Aeroplane Arms drill exaggerates the 'C' shape and helps with the timing and smoothness of the transition from one side to the other.

OFF-PISTE PERFORMANCE

Moving the poles so that they are parallel to the gradient of the slope on exiting the turn, to improve the 'C' shape and therefore have better balance over the outside ski.

Parallel Poles

This is an excellent drill to give the skier a visual indicator of 'C' shape. It encourages the body to exaggerate the movement, hence improving balance over the outside ski. Ski with your poles held out in front and aim to exit the turn with the poles parallel to the gradient of the slope. If they aren't parallel to the gradient of the slope, adjust them until they are. When you have done this drill and returned to off-piste skiing, you can imagine that you are holding a piece of string between your two hands and aim to get it parallel to the gradient of the slope, to improve balance over the outside ski.

"I was an experienced mountaineer and skier but had done very little skiing off-piste. With a desire for summits, I found myself, with skis, at the top of Gran Paradiso in January shouting "I've never really skied off-piste before" to my friends in front. The reply came "Keep your hand on your outside knee as you go round the corner". With my instinct to lean into the mountain being so powerful, this simple sole focus was my key to getting off the mountain before it got dark. It worked, and I quickly made progress down the mountain without falling over. Having a positive technical focus quickly ensured all the fears associated with the snow and terrain were pushed to the back of my mind. At the time I had no idea why I was being asked to do this, but now I understand that it was to keep me balancing over my outside ski."

BENDING AND STRETCHING

Bending and stretching the legs is a key movement for good balance through changing terrain and snow conditions. The full range of movement isn't always needed, but being familiar and well-practised with the range means it can be used whenever required.

What is bending and stretching?

This is the action of bending and stretching the legs to go from being tall to being short, and from short to tall, by using the ankle, knee and hip joints. This is also referred to as flexion and extension.

KEY MOVEMENTS

Bending and stretching of the legs using the ankle, knee and hip joints, to deal with the changing terrain off-piste.

Showing flexed legs in powder (photo ▼).

Fully flexed legs, to stay in balance over the bumps (photo ▶).

Why is this required off-piste?

It is important to be able to bend and stretch the legs in order to maintain balance through changes in terrain or snow consistency. For example, if the skis go into a big drift of powder and the legs stayed fixed in the same position, the skis will slow as the snow provides resistance and the body will continue at the same speed, resulting in an abrupt forward bend from the waist or, at worst, a forward face plant. By bending the legs on entering the deeper snow, the skis will start to accelerate through the resistance of the deeper snow, continuing at the same speed, with the body staying in balance over the skis.

Similarly, legs need to bend and stretch with changes in terrain, such as when going over bumps.

OFF-PISTE PERFORMANCE

Using shin and heel contact points to feel 'centred' on the skis.

How to do it well

Bending and stretching should use all three joints; ankles, knees and hips. It's much easier to bend and stretch these joints to their full extent when centred on the skis. What is meant by being 'centred'? Use the feeling of equal pressure on the shin and under the heel as a guide. The shin should be resting on the front of the boot, but not pressing. The heel of the foot should be pressing down into the ski, but not the calf muscle on the back of the boot. Too much pressure on the front of the boot indicates being forward of centre which inhibits bending and stretching. Lose contact with the front of the boot for too long and the likelihood is you are now back from centre and flexing the ankle joint will be challenging.

Here the skier is only bending from the waist. This can often occur when skiers look at their feet (photo ▲).

> "I had always focused on pressing my shins hard into the front of my boots, so much so that I had sore shins at the end of every day. Whenever I entered deep snow, I found myself face planting. By focusing on pressing the heel of my foot lightly down into the sole of my boot, I found that I was no longer face planting in powder. I had one of my best runs when I imagined that my binding was broken and I had to press down through my heel to keep my ski attached to my boot! My mantra is now 'shin and heel'."

Don't worry about the timing of bending and stretching within the turn. For off-piste skiing, the key is being able to do the movement and then the snow type and terrain will dictate when the movement should occur. Practise using a full range of movement so that maximum extent can be used if and when required. The faster you ski, the greater the range of movement that will be required to maintain control.

Smooth bending and stretching using the ankle, knee and hip joints, while feeling the shin touching the front of the boot and the heel pressing down through the sole of the boot. The skier is looking ahead throughout the full range of movement (photos ◤▶).

KEY MOVEMENTS

Squats on Skis

This is an excellent drill to exaggerate the action of bending and stretching, while being centred on the skis. Traverse across the slope and try to bend and stretch the legs as much as possible, going from being tall to small, and then small to tall. See if you can get your bottom to touch the back of your binding, while keeping the shin in contact with the front of the boot. Only go as far down as feels comfortable and make sure that you can get back up from the position! Notice how the skis will accelerate as you bend, this will be useful in powder where there is resistance from the snow. Play around with the rate and range of the movement, aiming to make it as smooth as possible. Look ahead to avoid too much flex coming from the hips. Primarily focus on bending the lower leg, as the upper leg will follow in unison and this will help maintain the 'C' shape and balance over the outside (lower) ski.

Practising bending and stretching using ankles, knees, and hips.

OFF-PISTE PERFORMANCE

Squats in Bumps

Try the same drill as 'Squats on Skis' but this time with some bumps in the way. The legs should bend as the skis are going up the bump and stretch as the skis are going down the other side, meaning that the legs are at their shortest on top of the bump and their longest in the trough. You can try this with your eyes closed, aiming to respond to the terrain by feeling what is happening under the skis.

Demonstrating good, smooth bending and stretching to balance effectively, while going over some bumps.

"After listening to the explanation of bending and stretching and watching a few demonstrations, I realised that in intimidating situations I tended to tense up and therefore block any movement of my legs, in just the place where I really needed maximum movement. And, as a result, the snow or change in terrain moved me out of balance. Now I relax and exaggerate the leg movement as I approach changes in terrain so I am not moved out of balance. My mantra simply became 'Move (yourself) or be moved (by the snow)'."

KEY MOVEMENTS

Flex or Face Plant
Find a place where the skis are initially on the surface of the snow and travel (either straight down the fall line or on a traverse) into some soft snow where the skis will disappear below the surface and go into the snow. Aim to maintain a constant speed as the skis go into the deeper snow. This will be achieved by bending the legs as the skis transition from being on top of the snow to being in the snow. An ideal venue for this is often going from a groomed slope into some powder at the edge of the piste.

This is an ideal venue for the Flex or Face Plant drill, with a groomed slope transitioning to powder. Aim to ski from the groomed slope into the powder while maintaining balance and not losing speed. This will be achieved by bending the legs using all three joints: ankles, knees and hips.

MOVING FORWARD INTO THE TURN

A committed movement, forward and downhill, is required with the body at the start of the turn. This is needed to stay in balance over the skis when the skis come into the fall line. It is particularly important when the terrain gets steeper. A movement forward needs to be made to initiate the turn, aiming to get the body perpendicular to the skis and slope when the skis are in the fall line.

Moving forward at the start of the turn, to stay in balance when the skis come into the fall line.

What is moving forward into the turn?
This is the action of letting the hips move in front, and across, the feet at the start of the turn.

OFF-PISTE PERFORMANCE

When the skis are perpendicular to the slope it's relatively easy to stand centred (shin and heel) over the skis. As the skis go into the turn and into the fall line the hips need to remain centred over the skis. For this to happen, the hips need to be moving forward prior to the turning action of the skis.

The skier has moved forward before the turn and as a result, the skier's body is perpendicular to the skis when in the fall line, making the skis easier to steer through the second half of the turn.

Leaning back when the skis are in the fall line makes it difficult to steer the skis through the second half of the turn. In fact, they have forgotten to move forward.

KEY MOVEMENTS

Why is this required off-piste?
Quite simply, if you don't move forward, you will end up back. This will result in an unwanted acceleration out of the turn and a loss of control of speed and direction. If you don't move forward into the turn there can also be an element of feeling the backs of the skis 'catching' as they are turned. This is most commonly felt in deep snow that the skis sink into, or on steeper ground.

The skier has actively moved forward at the start of the turn to ensure that their body is perpendicular to the slope when the skis are in the fall line, and as a result, the heels of the skis are free and come around easily.

How to do it well
Stand with the skis perpendicular to the slope, centred over the skis. While standing still, turn the skis into the fall line without moving the body position. Notice how the body is no longer perpendicular to the skis and the skis are hard to pivot through the final stages of the turn.

Now let's incorporate moving forward to feel the difference. Allow the upper hip bone to cross the skis at 45 degrees, to come over and in front of the feet before they turn. At this stage you will feel more 'shin' than heel. That's ok. Next, turn the skis into the fall line. This time the body will be perpendicular to the skis when in the fall line. As a result, the skis will be much easier to pivot through the final stages of the turn. More 'heel' will be felt at the end of the turn as the skis return to perpendicular to the slope.

This is an active, positive movement in which the body moves before the skis. When done well, the skis will start to turn as a result of the body movement. While it helps to focus on the hips to initiate the movement, don't let the hips overtake the head as the whole body needs to move forward.

OFF-PISTE PERFORMANCE

Diving In

This is an excellent drill to get a good grasp of the movement. Take your skis off and stand with your feet pointing across the slope, in a flexed position. Move the uphill hip bone up across the feet so that you almost topple forwards out of balance. The need to step forward to regain balance is an indicator that the movement has been done effectively.

Stages of the Diving In drill.

KEY MOVEMENTS

Superman

This is the same drill as diving in, but done with skis on. When it's done well and with commitment, it will feel like you are about to go down the slope headfirst on your tummy, but you won't. Exaggerate this movement on an easy piste and feel that the skis start to turn themselves as you make the movement. Notice how much body movement there is before the skis start to turn.

Stages of the Superman drill. Notice how much the body moves before the skis move.

> "On steeper slopes, I have a strong desire for my speed to be slow. But the more intimidated I became, the more I found my skis running away from me. After discovering the action of moving forward was essentially missing from my skiing, I understood why. Now, the more I project forward, the slower I can make my skis go! This was contradictory to what I had previously thought. I now launch my body downhill into the turn as I know it gives me the ability to go slower."

OFF-PISTE PERFORMANCE

Pole on Hips

This is a good drill to gain further feel for the action of moving forward into the turn. Stand with your skis perpendicular to the slope. Rest a ski pole gently against your hip bones. Aim to move the pole so that it is parallel with your lower ski, but without it losing contact with your hip bone. In order to do this, you will be moving forward into the turn. Notice that when you do the movement the tips of the skis start to turn into the fall line.

Gaining an awareness of moving forward into the turn by focusing on the movement of the hips.

"For a long time, I thought that I was leaning back at the end of the turn and, as hard as I tried, I couldn't fix it. I now realise that I wasn't leaning back, I had forgotten to move forward. This is much easier to fix, as now when I get the leaning back feeling, I project my hips forward into the next turn."

KEY MOVEMENTS

Heel catch

If the front of the inside ski is lifting off the snow this should be addressed as a priority. It is a common cause of knee injury as the back of the ski gets stuck in the snow, and increased force has to be used to bring the ski around. This becomes increasingly prevalent in heavy snow, and more force is required to bring the ski around, further increasing the risk of injury.

Front of the inside ski coming off the snow and as a result, the heel catches.

If the front of the inside ski is off the snow, focus on what it does to the tail of the ski. It anchors it deeper into the snow, making it harder to turn. As a result, the skier uses force to bring the ski around. The more the skier thinks it is catching, the more the skier tries to take the weight off the ski to get it around. Since the skier can only see the front of the ski they try to lift it further, causing the heel to dig in even more. This can be a sign that the skier has not moved forward into the turn. It can be solved by practising the drills for moving forward, or focusing on keeping the toes on the snow, which will in turn lighten the back of the ski. The overall aim is to have the toe on the snow, with the heel light but not lifted. However, it is better to lift the heel, than to have the tail of the ski catch.

OFF-PISTE PERFORMANCE

Toe on the Snow

When initiating the turn, lift the lower heel away from the surface of the snow and keep the front of the ski on the snow. Pointing the toes, and extending the ankle joint, will help to achieve this.

Lifting the heel as a drill to keep the toe on the snow.

TURNING

Thinking about how to use our hips, legs and feet to initiate different types of turns.

There are two main ways in which skis can be turned, by twisting and by edging. Both are equally important and give considerably different outcomes. In order to be proficient at skiing off-piste you need to be competent at both. The more you understand when to twist and when to edge, the better you will become at blending edging and twisting according to the prevailing snow conditions and terrain, and the more skilful you will be off-piste. There are situations where edging will work effectively and twisting will not, and vice versa. Equally, there are situations where both will work well.

Think of this as a spectrum with twisting at one end and edging at the other. In the majority of cases on-piste, skiers move around the hill doing a turn which uses some twisting and some edging, somewhere in the middle of the spectrum.

The twisting and edging spectrum. The majority of turns that skiers do are somewhere in the middle, which works well in the majority of cases, but not when conditions become challenging.

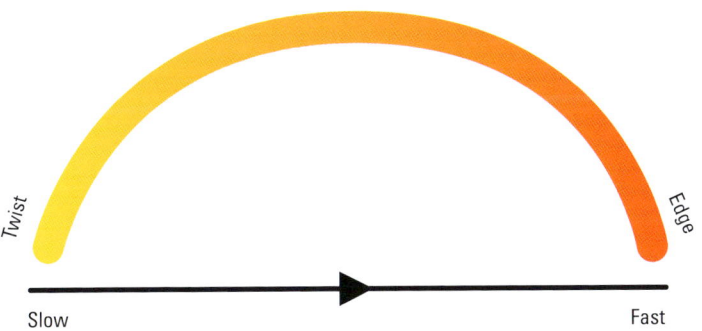

OFF-PISTE PERFORMANCE

Off-piste skiers should aim to be skilled at the extreme ends of the spectrum, and everything in between, to have boundless options for dealing with a variety of conditions.

In both twisting and edging, the skier aims to make the same movement with both feet at the same time. The exception to this is when using a snowplough. In this case, the outside ski will twist and edge before the inside one.

Skiers have a natural tendency to be better at either edging or twisting, and this often depends on when and how they learned to ski. Those that learned to ski before the development of carving skis generally have a preference towards twisting, as that was the most effective way to turn the skis. Those that learned on carving skis are usually better at edging. With the arrival of carving skis came the onset of the myth that twisting skis was bad and it was often frowned upon. Twisting the skis is good and is an essential part of skiing off-piste. Ski design has had a huge influence on the way we ski. Or has the way we ski influenced ski design? Do we go faster because the skis let us, or did we want to go faster so skis were developed to allow that? In reality, it's most likely a bit of both.

History of ski design

There is evidence of ski use from over 5,000 years ago in Arctic regions, with findings of rock paintings depicting skis and ski remnants found as glaciers have retreated. The first skis were made of wood, mostly ash, which is both strong and springy. Ash is still used in ski manufacturing today.

The earliest known use of skis was to travel for hunting purposes. Later, armies used skis for training and competitions long before the idea of skiing as recreation arrived in the mid 19th century.

Significant developments in ski design also came in the mid 19th century when the concept of camber was introduced by woodcarvers in the Norwegian province of Telemark. Prior to skis having a camber, a skier would often find themselves sinking into a hole in the snow due to the pressure exerted directly under the feet, causing the ski to turn upwards at either end and sink in the middle. Giving the ski a camber, a bow shape that rises in the middle, spreads the weight of the skier more evenly along the ski, making the ski float better and turn more easily.

The idea of grooming slopes in preparation for skiing didn't arise until a century later, so all skis were designed for what today we know as 'off-piste'.

Around a decade after the notion of camber was introduced, Sondre Norheim from Telemark developed side cut, the idea of narrowing the middle of the ski to allow it to turn more easily. The dimensions of Norheim's skis were around 81-67-70, resulting in a turn radius of 83 metres. By comparison, 30 metres would be considered a large turning radius by today's standards.

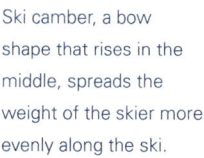

Ski camber, a bow shape that rises in the middle, spreads the weight of the skier more evenly along the ski.

Steel edges arrived in the 1920s, with the first designs coming from Austria. In early designs, the metal segments tended to come loose while skiing, so spare segments, screws and a screwdriver had to be carried to make repairs on the mountain. Most advances in ski design over the next 50 years focused primarily on materials, rather than shape.

In 1984, there was a request from an executive in America for a ski that would make learning easier. Frank Meatto designed a ski with the dimensions 128-40-79, giving a turn radius of 8m. This was a dramatic shift from anything available on the market at that time. The ski was called 'Albert' after the designer's dog's toy and 150 pairs were produced. Ski instructors were enthusiastic but retailers thought the dramatic shape would not sell and hence the ski quietly disappeared off the scene. There is speculation that ski manufacturer Kneissl may have seen the 'Albert' designs from 1984 as their ownership ended up in the hands of the executive that had requested the easy-to-learn ski.

Snowboards arrived on the snow sports scene in the 1970s and many ski manufacturers were now making snowboards too. When Atomic were asked to produce a powder ski in 1988, they simply sawed a snowboard in half and put bindings on it, making a ski that was 115mm underfoot.

During the 1990s Elan and Kneissl built prototypes of shaped 'carving' skis, moving from the original Telemark geometry towards a generation of easy-to-turn skis which became known as 'parabolic' skis. Salomon famously stalled the carving revolution for a few years when they entered the ski market with their capped skis, but it wasn't long before parabolic skis dominated the market.

In the early 2000s skis with rocker were introduced. Now, with camber, side cut and rocker, the possible combinations are infinite, hence there is an extensive range of skis on the market. It will be interesting to see how ski design evolves over the next 50 years. The current focus seems to centre around making tough skis from lighter materials and making more environmentally sustainable products.

TWISTING

Twisting is the action of turning your foot to turn the ski. It can come from ankle and hip joints, and also the whole body. This twisting action is often referred to as rotation or pivoting. The action is the same, the feet will remain in a similar spot, and the tips and the tails of the skis will follow a completely different path. The tracks that are left in the snow from turns that are predominantly twisting will be roughly 'Z' shaped, (in contrast, the tracks left in the snow from turns that are predominantly edging will be roughly 'S' shaped).

OFF-PISTE PERFORMANCE

Understand the movement

Dancing

Stand without skis on a firm surface with your feet hip width apart. Use poles for balance to make the feet light. Try to keep the centre of your foot in the same place and move your toes in one direction and your heels in the other. The aim is for the movement to be centred around the middle of the foot. Look at the pattern left in the snow. Notice that the foot needs to be flat on the snow for it to be twisted.

Practising the twisting motion without skis on.

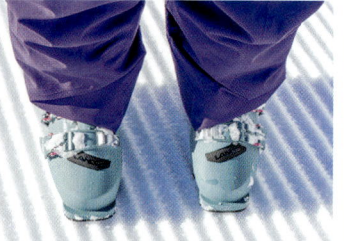

No Tracks

Aim for the edges of your skis to leave no tracks of their own in the snow and cover up any existing tracks as you go. This can only be done using a twisting motion.

The feet have remained in a similar spot with the tips and the tails of the skis following a completely different path. The edges of the skis leave no distinct tracks in the snow, smoothing over any existing tracks on the way.

Pros

- Gives the ability to turn in a very small space.
- Gives the ability to turn without gathering much, or any speed.
- Easy to do when skis are on the surface of the snow.
- It can be done in the air.
- Less space is required when coming to a stop.

Cons

- Hard to do if your skis are 'in' the snow, as opposed to 'on' the snow.
- It is time-consuming. You will end up doing a lot of turns but not cover much ground!
- Possible to overbalance or catch an edge if done at speed.

TURNING

Practise the movement

This drill isolates the movement beneath the waist, so the movement can become independent of the upper body. Feel that the movement can come from both the ankle joint and from the hip rotating within its socket.

Skis in the Air

Lie on your back with skis in the air. Keep your feet in the same place and turn the tips and the tails in opposite directions. Notice that the twist can come from the ankle joint, but also from the hip turning within the hip socket. Watch and observe if both skis are moving at the same time and in sync with each other. Try it with the skis close together and far apart. Which do you find easier?

Aim for the skis to change direction without the feet moving away from the line drawn in the snow.

Twist on a Line

Ask a partner to draw a line in the snow, going down the slope. Aim to make turns down the slope with your feet staying on, or near, the line. This will replicate the idea of skiing in a narrow couloir. Firstly, let the ski bases come flat against the snow, then twist the feet to turn. Check where your feet are in relation to the line. Your partner can give feedback on how much your feet deviated from the line during the turns.

OFF-PISTE PERFORMANCE

Poles Downhill

Hold your poles horizontally in front of you. Now do some short turns going down the slope, aiming to keep the poles facing towards the bottom of the hill. This will encourage a twisting action from the lower body, not the whole body, making the movement more efficient. This is known as rotational separation since the upper body is separating with a rotary movement from the lower body.

Encouraging the twisting action to come from the lower body and not the whole body, by keeping the poles facing towards the camera. Although the upper body looks still throughout this drill, the upper body is in fact moving left as the lower body moves right, and right as the lower body moves left, to maintain facing down the hill. Done correctly, it will feel like there is a lot of rotational movement around the middle of the body.

"I had always strived to carve my skis, thinking that rotating the skis across their path was bad. When introduced to twisting, I realised that this was a movement I was very familiar with, but I had actively been trying to avoid doing it. It was no wonder that I seemed to struggle on steep, bumpy or narrow terrain. I now allow myself to twist the skis and I can turn easily in a really small space."

TURNING

EDGING

Edging is the action of rolling the skis onto their edges by using the ankle joint, hip joint and the whole body. Carving is the word used to describe the action of edging through the whole turn, where the whole ski follows the same path for the duration of the turn. The key for off-piste is the timing of the edge change, striving to have the ability to do it as early as possible in the turn. A turn that is predominantly edging will be 'S' shaped. Edging will be most effective if the lower legs are parallel to each other, and both feet make the same action at the same time.

Understand the movement

Big Toe, Little Toe

Stand without your skis on and roll from balancing on one big toe and one little toe, to the other little toe and big toe. The feet will not turn in this situation but will roll from one edge to another. Next, try this with skis on using a gentle slope. Let the skis run down the fall line. Just by rolling the skis from one edge to the other, the skis will deviate from the fall line. It will feel like you are making a movement which results in the skis turning, rather than consciously trying to turn the skis.

Rolling from one edge to the other, from big toe to little toe.

OFF-PISTE PERFORMANCE

Tracks

Stand with your skis flat, pointing straight down a gentle slope. Let them run and once the skis are in motion, tilt the skis onto their edges (but without twisting the feet). Let the skis continue to curve around until they start to point uphill and come to a stop. Look back at your tracks. Are there two clean, parallel lines in the snow? If so, this is a turn that has used only edging. If not, repeat until there are two clean, parallel lines. Repeat in both directions.

Leaving two clean, parallel tracks, turning by rolling the skis onto their edges.

TURNING

Pros

- Feels effortless when done correctly.
- Ability to cover a lot of ground with fewer turns.
- It can be fast and you can gather speed while turning.
- It can be done if skis are 'in' the snow, or 'on' the snow.
- It can be done in the air.

Cons

- It can be fast and you can gather speed while turning.
- Requires a larger turning area than twisting.
- More time and space are needed to slow down and stop.

Practise the movement

Hand Inside

Place one hand on the outside of the inside knee. This helps to ensure that the inside ski is edged the same amount as the outside ski, as often the inside ski gets forgotten about. Have the other arm outstretched to remember the body 'C' shape. Look back at your tracks and ensure that both skis do the same thing at the same time.

Using one hand to assist with edging the inside ski and the other to assist with maintaining a 'C' shape and balance over the outside ski.

OFF-PISTE PERFORMANCE

Little Edge, Lots of Edge

Experiment with tilting the edges a little and a lot, and feel the different outcomes. Using a little edge, the skis will take longer to come around, use a lot of edge and the skis will come around quicker. For little edge, imagine that it's just enough room for a piece of paper to be slid under the skis. For a lot of edge, imagine creating enough room for a brick to be slid under the skis. When using a lot of edge, more 'C' shape will be needed to balance effectively.

Using a little edge tilt and lots of edge tilt.

"I was starting to get the feel for the movement of edging when I found myself consistently falling into the mountain as I rolled the skis onto their edges. I realised that I was rolling the skis onto the edges using my whole body and forgetting the importance of the 'C' shape! A little tilt back with the body was required to stay in balance. My mantra is 'edges in, body out'."

The key movements and the ways of turning can be varied to create significantly different outputs. The rate of movement (how fast), range of movement (how much) and the timing of the movement (when) can vary, and in all cases the aim is to have smooth movements.

Pressure

Pressure is a term that is often associated with skiing but can cause lots of confusion. Pressure is the term that skiers use to describe the force that a skier exerts on the snow. The force passes through the body and skis onto the snow. Pressure is always present in skiing but is not visible, although the effects of pressure can be seen, heard and felt. Pressure can be applied to the skis, and once pressure has been applied, it then needs to be managed.

It's worth noting that pressure can be applied in different directions. Pressure can be applied downwards through the ski to the snow. For example, stand on the flat with both skis flat against the surface of the snow. Sink down and then extend upwards. Pressure has been applied in a vertical direction.

Pressure can also be applied horizontally. Think of a snowplough machine moving snow and then compare this to a skier's snowplough action moving snow sideways. In this case, pressure is being applied horizontally as the snow is pushed out of the way.

One of the risks of talking about pressure in off-piste skiing is that the skier presses hard through the skis causing the skis to sink, or the legs become straight and locked so unable to bend and stretch appropriately. Therefore, a better approach is to focus on the three key movements (see previous chapter), and make sure that they are done well and smoothly. Then the pressure will be applied and managed appropriately, without having to think about pressure application or management.

DIFFERENT TYPES OF SNOW

Ewan Stewart embracing deep, untracked powder.

One of the delights, but also one of the challenges, of off-piste skiing is the variability of the snow. The variability requires a constant need to adapt skills to achieve optimum performance. Weather has a dramatic influence on the snow. As the temperature, humidity and wind change, so do the snow conditions under the skis. Similarly, when skiing different aspects and gradients, and descending the mountain, the snow conditions will vary. While skiers relish the thought of some of these snow conditions, others can present significant challenges.

Anticipating the variations in snow conditions is key to being able to adapt skills accordingly. The snow conditions are very unlikely to be similar all the way down one off-piste descent. For example, you may set off down a wide, open and exposed area where the wind has impacted the snow. As you travel into a more sheltered spot, the snow becomes light, fluffy powder. Next, you cross a section that has had more direct sun, and the powder becomes heavier to ski. Then at lower elevations, it has rained and then frozen, causing a light crust to form on top of the snow. At the end of your descent, the snow becomes heavy and slushy. In this one descent, the key movements and ways of turning need to be varied significantly to match the changes in snow conditions. There is no set formula for skiing each type of snow, but rather an exploration of varying the ways of turning and subtle adjustments to the key movements to find what gives you optimal performance.

OFF-PISTE PERFORMANCE

The type of skis you have play a part in how enjoyable or challenging certain snow conditions will be. Skis can't be changed halfway down a run, but skills can!

Some preparation for the variability can be done while travelling uphill, whether it be with skins or using the lifts, by making continual observations. Has it been windy? Which slopes are in the sun and which are in the shade? If you are skinning, you can feel the snow to get an idea of how it will be to ski, although remember that it may change by the time you come to descend.

The most significant factor to consider is whether your skis will be 'on' or 'in' the snow, as this will influence whether a predominantly twisty or edgy turn will be more appropriate.

The following types of snow are not an exhaustive list, as the possible variations are endless. However, most forms of snow will fit into one of these categories, even though there is potential for significant variations. For example, powder can come in many different depths and densities. Nevertheless, the principles given will be helpful for all variations found within that category.

HARD-PACKED SNOW

On hard-packed or firm snow the skis are most definitely 'on' the snow. Skiing on hard-packed snow is essentially the same as skiing on a firm piste, but the snow has become compacted because of weather influences, such as wind and the traffic of skiers, rather than a piste machine. It is included here first as it is one of the easiest types of snow to ski off-piste, along with spring snow which follows next, and both can be a great way to progress from piste to off-piste skiing.

Different forms of hard-packed snow off-piste. The clear similarity in each situation is that the skis are on the surface of the snow, rather than being in the snow.

DIFFERENT TYPES OF SNOW

A dusting of fresh snow on top of a hard-packed base is a great opportunity for an introduction to making fresh tracks.

Enjoying the space with a dusting of fresh snow on a firm base.

Using space, when the skis are on the surface of the snow, to practise and play.

Practice ground

Skiing on hard-packed snow is an excellent opportunity to practise the three key movements and experiment with some twisty turns and some edgy turns. It's a good place to do a few drills that you've previously done on the piste. It's also an opportunity to check that you are looking ahead and not looking down at your skis. This can often be a better training ground than the piste, as there are normally fewer people so there is more space to practise.

Hard-packed snow with a light dusting of powder is another wonderful practice ground. The skis will be on the surface of the snow and there is an opportunity to make fresh tracks.

Boundless

The key difference between piste and hard-packed snow off-piste is that there are no marker poles to provide a boundary. View this as an opportunity rather than a hindrance. On-piste, the rhythm and route are often dictated by other skiers, whereas this is an opportunity to have more freedom over where you turn, not being restricted by the size of the piste, or by other people getting in your way. Vary your run according to what you want to do, be creative and enjoy the space.

Reduce the judder

One of the common problems on hard-packed snow is that skis, particularly the lower ski, judder through the end of the turn. This is often enhanced if skiing on lightweight touring skis. The judder is a sign that there is too much pressure coming on abruptly at the end of the turn, and the pressure is not being managed appropriately.

Aim to reduce the judder: there are a number of ways in which this can be done. Firstly, try simply tuning into the sound of the turn, which when juddering can often be unpleasant. Try

OFF-PISTE PERFORMANCE

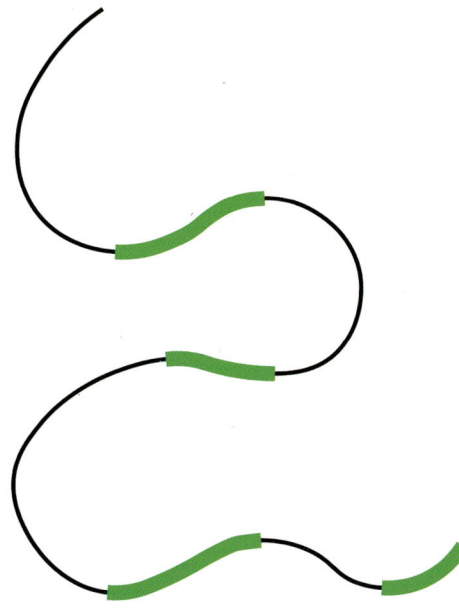

Let the skis turn up the hill to reduce speed, rather than slamming on the brakes.

to smooth out the sound and keep the volume the same throughout the whole turn. This in itself can mean that changes are made automatically, without having to think about what those adjustments are, with the focus being much more on the output than the input.

Next, think back to the key movement of balancing on the outside ski. The earlier in the turn that you can balance on the outside ski, the less judder there will be. Balance on the outside ski before you go round the turn, rather than as, or after, you turn. To balance on the outside ski early, gently press under the ball of the foot at the start of the turn. Feel like you are pressing the ski down into the snow, to get it to grip before going round the corner, and even before the ski changes onto its new edge. Press first, edge second.

The judder can also result from an abrupt desire to slow down after the turn, likened to slamming on the brakes. Instead, let the skis turn up the hill to manage the speed, giving a much smoother and softer end to the turn.

Everything that happens at the end of the turn is the outcome of what did, or didn't, happen at the start of the turn.

Core Strength

Skiing on hard-packed snow is a good place to think about body tension, in preparation for other snow types which may appear further down the same run. Aim for a relaxed yet anticipative stance, with some tension in the core muscles but without this extending to the legs.

Skier is relaxed but with their core engaged, focused and anticipating what will come next.

DIFFERENT TYPES OF SNOW

Fresh tracks in spring snow.

SPRING SNOW

Skiers enjoying spring snow in a variety of different places, with the skis on the surface of the snow, but with the snow being soft enough that there is some snow displacement.

Spring snow is a well-consolidated snowpack that has gone through numerous freeze-thaw cycles. The skis will be mostly on the snow, but as the snow softens the skis will sink further into the snow. Spring snow can be one of the most enjoyable types of snow to ski and again is very much like a piste. As a result, skiers rarely struggle with this type of snow. The surface can have a delightful velvety texture which allows skiers to make fresh tracks without the skis disappearing deep into the snow, again being a good introduction to off-piste.

This skier has had perfect spring snow near the top of the slope, but it has become heavier as they descended and the skis are sinking further into the snow, highlighted by the amount of snow spraying up from the skis.

Timing

Timing is key to ensuring spring snow is fun to ski. If you arrive too early in the day the snow will be firm and icy, and the skis will most definitely be on the surface of the snow. Arrive too late in the day and the snow will have turned to slush and the skis will sink into the snow. Get the timing just right and the surface layer of the snow will have softened just enough that your skis leave tracks in the snow, but don't sink into it.

If you arrive at your chosen descent too early and the snow is still icy, consider waiting until the snow has softened to get the timing just right. Use the time as an opportunity to have a rest, a bite to eat, and take in the view. Remember, you are unlikely to get perfect spring snow for the whole descent, so plan to get the timing right for the key sections of the run, for example, the steepest part.

Personal reflection

On the 20th of March 2015, our short visit to the Dolomites was coming to an end. We only had the morning available to ski, before making the long journey back to Chamonix. A descent of Couloir Joel was on our tick list and the morning looked perfect. It was to be a clear sunny day and the sun would come round to our slope mid-morning. This would be ideal timing to ski the couloir, with the spring snow starting to soften.

We took the Pordoi cable car and were surprised by the number of tourists on the viewing platform at the top, seemingly focused on something specific, but we couldn't identify what it was. As we made our way round to the top of the couloir, we did comment that the sun didn't seem as strong or bright as we'd expected, yet the sky was still clear.

On arriving at the top of the couloir, the sun had come round and was on the upper slopes, just as we had anticipated. We threw some snowballs down the upper part and were surprised that no indent was made in the snow. The couloir was clearly still icy and didn't look like an inviting place to ski. We decided to sit and wait for the snow to soften. After waiting a little while, we threw some more snow down the slope, and the same thing happened. The snowballs once again rattled down the icy slope. Feeling perplexed and frustrated, as we were adamant that our timing was right, we decided not to ski the couloir since it wasn't softening. We retreated to the car by an easier route, disappointed that we hadn't been able to ski our objective, but comfortable in our decision not to ski the couloir in those conditions.

On arriving back in Chamonix and catching up with the news, we discovered that the day had been a solar eclipse. We had been completely unaware of this and had not factored it into our planning!

DIFFERENT TYPES OF SNOW

Vary and exaggerate

Spring snow can be skied with edgy turns or twisty turns. It can be skied fast or slow. It can be skied in a narrow corridor or using the full width of the slope. Avoid getting stuck in your preferred turn shape and size. It is an opportunity to practise turn shapes and sizes that you use less often. You can get away with most things on spring snow, so ensure that you don't become lazy. It is a chance to exaggerate the key movements ready for when they are required. You'll also get more enjoyment that way, as the skis will become more responsive.

Constant speed

Aim to have a constant speed from one turn to the next. Imagine you have a speedometer on you. It doesn't matter if it's reading 15 miles per hour or 40 miles per hour, but it should read roughly the same around each turn rather than feeling like there is a stop–start motion. The moment at which you turn when achieving constant speed is often referred to as the sweet spot. Achieving this becomes hugely beneficial when skiing powder.

ICY SNOW

Skiing on icy snow can be noisy and unpleasant. Thankfully it can often be seen by the colour of the snow and therefore sometimes avoided altogether. If it can be avoided, then it should be. On ice, the skis will be on the surface of the snow.

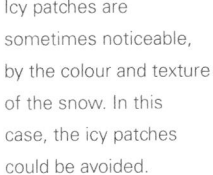

Icy patches are sometimes noticeable, by the colour and texture of the snow. In this case, the icy patches could be avoided.

OFF-PISTE PERFORMANCE

Slide gracefully

Sliding gracefully diagonally downhill is a great way to make progress down an icy slope, while limiting the number of turns required. This is essentially side slipping with continual motion, using a smooth twisty turn, when and if a change in direction is needed. Aim to lose as much height as possible through the slide after each turn, ensuring turns are linked with a slide downhill, rather than a traverse. Having a lower centre of gravity can feel more stable when sliding. A good 'C' shape is critical to feel that the slide can be done both positively and gracefully.

Making progress down an icy section with a graceful slide. Notice the pronounced 'C' shape to stay balanced over the lower ski.

Twists

When a turn is required, make it a twisty one. This will ensure that minimum speed is gained through the turn and that the majority of the travelling is done through the slide, rather than the turn, which can give greater stability.

Smooth movements

Movements on ice should be slow, smooth and subtle, avoiding any sudden and dramatic movements. The key movement to focus on is being well balanced over the outside ski, making a smooth and gentle transition from balancing on one ski to the other.

Using an appropriate edge angle for a slow and controlled descent on an icy slope.

Less edge, more grip

There is a common myth that when skiing on ice more edge is required to get the skis to slow down. In fact, there are two potential negative consequences of tilting the skis further on the edges. Firstly, the skis may slide out from underneath you. Secondly, edging the skis without any twisting action causes the skis to accelerate round a corner, at exactly the moment you want the skis to slow down.

Aim to ski on ice with flatter skis to maximise the grip. Resist the urge to edge more. Try imagining that you don't want anyone to see the bases of your skis as you descend an icy slope.

DIFFERENT TYPES OF SNOW

POWDER

Fresh snow, that has fallen with little or no wind, is most experienced off-piste skiers' dream. Equally, it can be the inexperienced skier's worst nightmare, quickly becoming physically draining and mentally exhausting. Skied well, there is a real sense of achievement leaving perfect tracks, your mark on the previously untouched mountainside. Even within one powder field many variables may exist, such as the depth and density of the powder, and in turn, the optimal way of skiing the slope will vary. In powder, the skis will most definitely be 'in' the snow.

Freshly fallen cold powder snow is a proficient off-piste skier's dream.

The myths

There are a couple of myths surrounding powder skiing. Unfortunately, many skiers attempt powder skiing with these as a focus, striving to achieve them, not realising that they are hindering performance. The first myth is that the skis need to be close together. Powder can be skied successfully with skis close together or far apart. Generally, this will depend on the overall speed. If powder is being skied fast, the skis will be further apart to aid stability. If the skier opts for a slower speed, then the skis may be closer together. Skiers with fatter skis often opt for a wider stance to avoid the skis touching. Conversely, skiers with narrower skis may choose to use a narrow stance, to create one platform with the skis. Hip width apart is an ideal platform to aim for.

Skiers being successful, and having fun, in powder with varying widths of stance. The chap with the narrow stance summed up his performance by saying "You don't need to look like a hero to feel like one!" It's far better to focus on what your skiing feels like, than what it looks like.

OFF-PISTE PERFORMANCE

The second myth is that the weight of the skier needs to be spread equally over both skis. Think back to the key movement of balancing over the outside ski. If travelling straight down the mountain the weight will be spread equally over both skis, but as the skis deviate from the fall line there is a need to balance over the outside ski, irrespective of the snow type. Many powder skiers take a direct line down the fall line due to the resistance of the snow slowing their speed, hence their weight will be distributed equally over both skis. However, when faced with a steep powder field, or simply a desire to turn the skis perpendicular to the fall line, then balance needs to be maintained over the outside ski. 'Balance' is a key word. Interpret this as 'press' and the ski will sink deep into the powder, 'balance' and the skis will float through it.

Balancing over both skis whilst skiing direct down the fall line (photo ▼).

Balancing more over the outside ski when deviating from the fall line, as shown by the 'C' shape created with the body (photo ◥).

Avoid putting too much emphasis on either width of stance, or balance between skis. Instead, pay attention to one of the factors below, giving a positive focus to improve performance.

Flotation

The most important objective in powder is to get the skis floating. This means that the tips of the skis are coming to, or near, the surface and the skis maintain momentum through the snow. There needs to be an element of speed to achieve this. To feel comfortable with speed, balance is key. This means ensuring all of the key movements are refined, paying particular attention to bending and stretching. Look at the three photos at the top of the next page. The first and second skiers are getting the tips out of the snow by leaning back with relatively straight legs and little ankle flex. Their thighs are burning and their control while turning has been compromised. The third skier has got the tips of the skis to come out of the snow by flexing hips, knees and ankles. They have maintained 'shin and heel' contact and will be able to steer the skis effectively. Sometimes in powder, simply focusing on lifting your toes in your boots, helps to achieve shin and heel contact and aids flotation.

Focusing on when to turn, instead of where to turn, can aid flotation in powder. If focusing on where to turn, often momentum has dropped by the time the place has been reached, making starting a new turn challenging.

DIFFERENT TYPES OF SNOW

Leaning back in powder with tired legs and little control (photos ▲ ◤).

Skier balanced over the shin and heel and able to control the skis (photo far ◤).

Try shifting the focus to when to turn. The 'when' should be at the moment the speed has been controlled, but not stalled, often referred to as the sweet spot. It is normally a fraction of a second sooner than you think, or would like! Counting through the turn is a good way to achieve turning at the sweet spot. Count "1, 2, 3 and turn" out loud.

Flotation

Point the skis across the slope and let the skis glide, making your own tracks across the slope in the powder, not following in the tracks of others. Feel that the resistance of the snow starts to slow the skis. Bend and stretch the legs and feel the impact that this has on resistance and speed. As confidence increases, do this closer to the fall line to become comfortable with higher speed. This is a great drill for the first time in powder, and also a good warm-up for experienced skiers to get a handle on the depth and density of the powder before the first turn. Remember, speed is your friend in powder.

Demonstrating the Flotation drill.

OFF-PISTE PERFORMANCE

Blending twisting and edging

We know from the chapter on turning that when the skis are twisting they generate very little speed, hence this hinders flotation. Edging the skis will cause the skis to generate speed around the curve, which is what is needed in powder to aid flotation. If you twist the skis from the fall line to perpendicular in powder the skis will stall, with the skier most likely to go over the front of them. Twist the skis a little and some speed will be maintained, or edge them around the full curve if you want to go faster. Look at the diagram showing the variations below.

The path of the skis on the left is twisting and will not work effectively in powder. The path of the skis in the middle shows a blend of twisting and edging and is effective in powder, as is the path of the skis on the right showing an edged turn.

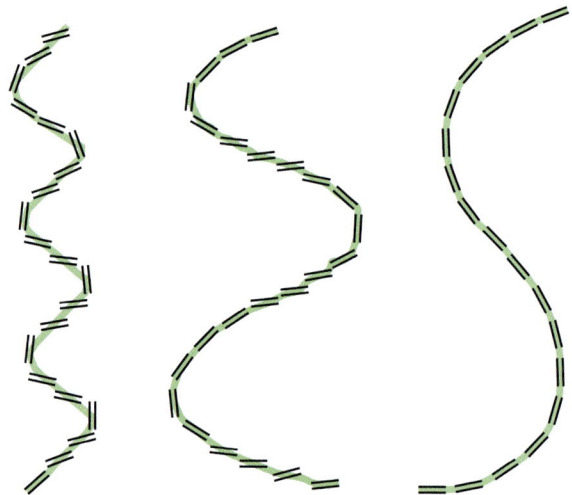

Both skis moving together

Aspire to have both skis moving together. To achieve this there needs to be good balance over the outside ski. Without this, the inside ski can become blocked and unable to move. When balanced over the outside ski, the inside ski will feel free and able to move in sync with the outside one.

To improve the ability to move both skis together, return to the balancing over the outside ski drills, and try these in powder too.

The skier is in a blocked position and is unable to move both skis together. They may feel lots of 'pressure' through the outside ski because the leg is long and outstretched, but they are balanced on the inside one, which is blocked underneath them.

DIFFERENT TYPES OF SNOW

The skier is able to move both skis together, or independently if they choose, because they are balanced over the outside ski and the inside one can move freely.

Bounce

Sometimes powder can be light enough that it feels 'bouncy' to ski. This is much more to do with the density and depth of the snow than any techniques used. Try traversing across the powder whilst bending and stretching the legs. If there starts to be a rebound, much like the feeling on a trampoline, then this can be incorporated into the turns. Link the timing of the bounce to the pole plant and you'll start to do bouncy turns. Pole planting can really aid performance in powder, helping with both bounce and rhythm.

Bouncy snow, although it's hard to tell from a photo, you know the snow is bouncy from the spray and the smile! Appropriate pole carriage to help aid balance and bounce, while staying centred over the skis.

Turn, Turn, Turn

This drill will help aid both flotation and rhythm. Ask an experienced off-piste skier to follow you down the slope. Initiate your own first turn, but after that turn on the command of the skier behind you. They should watch carefully and observe for the 'sweet spot', where your speed is under control, but has not started to decelerate. They will shout the command 'turn' at this key point. If you are getting faster and faster down the slope then the command is too early, ahead of the sweet spot. If you feel the skis start to decelerate, then the command is too late. Feel like you have a constant speed, then the command is just right. Ignore their call if you feel uncomfortable, or spot an obstacle in front.

OFF-PISTE PERFORMANCE

Wind affected snow

Snow can fall with wind, and it can also be moved by the wind after the snowfall. In both situations, snow that has been affected by the wind can be anything from easy to very challenging to ski. The snow's characteristics will depend on many factors, including how strong the wind has been and where the wind has come from. For example, the wind can strip fresh snow off areas facing into the wind, exposing bare ground or snow that is compacted and firm. In this case the skis will remain 'on' the snow. The snow that has been moved will be deposited in sheltered locations and can be soft and feel powdery to ski, with the skis being 'in' the snow. The wind can also cause a crust to form on the snow, resulting in either breakable or supporting crust, where the skis will sometimes be 'on' the snow and sometimes 'in' the snow.

Wind affected snow is a common occurrence in Scotland, and with a positive approach and adaptable skills it can be enjoyable.
📷 Andy Townsend

Golf-ball snow

Golf-ball snow, as it has affectionately become known, is a type of snow that has been very lightly affected by the wind and it is great fun to ski. It's easily recognisable as it looks dimpled, like the surface of a golf ball. It often occurs as patches in amongst much denser snow, and it can be a relief and welcome break when you see it. If you see it, ski it, as it will be preferable to the snow surrounding it.

Golf-ball snow (photo ▼).

Staying on the surface of hard-packed, wind affected snow (photo ▶).

DIFFERENT TYPES OF SNOW

Chopped-up powder.

CHOPPED-UP POWDER

After a lot of skiers have skied the powder in the same area it will become chopped up, leaving pockets of untracked snow, lumps where the snow has been pushed together by the skiers, and troughs in between, resulting in an incredibly variable surface. Sometimes the skis will be 'on' the snow and sometimes they will be 'in' the snow. You might even find that one ski is on the surface of the snow, whilst the other ski is in it! Chopped-up powder is what you will find by mid-morning on a cold January powder day at Les Grands Montets resort in the Chamonix Valley, an area famed for its off-piste.

Chopped-up powder presents a different challenge to fresh powder, with many skiers referring to the snow as being 'tracked out' in a negative sense. However, it can still be lots of fun to ski and can provide an equally rewarding challenge to skiing fresh, untracked powder.

Chopped-up powder.

OFF-PISTE PERFORMANCE

Tips level

Bending and stretching is key to dealing with the constant changes in terrain and snow consistency. Bending and stretching will be achieved most effectively if the tips of the skis are level when, and if, the skis come perpendicular to the fall line. There is a strong tendency in this type of snow to come perpendicular to the hill to help control speed, as there isn't the same resistance from the snow as in fresh powder.

Tips Level

Stand with your uphill ski in front of the downhill one. Notice that there will be lots of pressure on your lower shin, but very little on the heel. The lower leg is locked in a fixed position and it is challenging to flex it. Now stand with the tips of the skis level and feel that it is much easier to bend and stretch. Traverse across a slope playing with having the tips of the skis level, and separated. Try to bend and stretch as much as possible in each position and observe the differences. Try and identify when the tips of the skis are level with your eyes closed.

The skier is finding it challenging to use their full range of bending and stretching, and is in a less stable position. Daylight can be seen between the two legs, an indication that the split is too great to balance effectively.

The skier is able to use their full range of bending and stretching to absorb changes in terrain and is in a more stable position. The upper body is following the direction of momentum.

DIFFERENT TYPES OF SNOW

 Pull Over

This is a very useful drill to get the feeling for having the ski tips level and also for enforcing 'C' shape. Stand on a slope, firstly with your uphill ski in front of the downhill one. Ask a partner to try and pull you over, whilst standing below you. You will most likely find that they can pull you off balance relatively easily. Next, stand with the tips of your skis level. You should find that you are now in a much stronger position to resist the pull of your partner. This is a powerful ski position. You will also notice that your upper body moves over the outside ski to stay in balance, creating a "C" shape with your body.

The skier has their uphill ski in front of the downhill ski and is easily pulled off balance by their partner (photo ▶).

The skier is in a powerful position, with the tips of their skis level, and is able to resist the pull of their partner. The body is facing across the hill, the stance is hip width apart and the body is in a 'C' shape to stay in balance over the outside ski (photo far ◀).

The path of the outside ski is further than the path of the inside one.

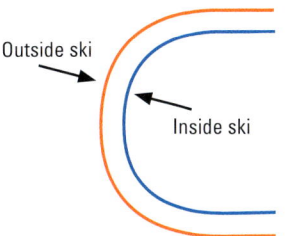

The separation in the tips of the skis occurs primarily because the outside ski has further to travel than the inside ski around the turn, resulting in the outside ski lagging behind when exiting the turn.

Level skis can be achieved by pushing the outside ski forward coming around the turn, pulling the inside ski back, or a bit of both. Skiers who have telemarked can liken it to the feeling of a telemark turn. Letting the body follow the skis will also help the tips of the skis to be level. Notice that when the ski tips are level, only one leg is visible when you look at the skier side on.

Tips level is for coming out of the turn, not starting the turn. As you start the turn, you may actively drive the outside ski forward to ensure it gets around the path of the turn quicker and comes out of the turn level to the uphill ski.

OFF-PISTE PERFORMANCE

Width of stance

A stance that is around hip width apart is key to maintaining balance in chopped-up powder. If the legs are too far apart the skis may travel through different terrain. One ski may be stopping in some powder whilst the other is accelerating through a tracked area. If the legs are too close together it is harder to balance and bend and stretch effectively. Aim for a stance width that is stable at speed, but where both skis travel over the same terrain and snow type.

Using an appropriate width of stance (hip width) in chopped-up powder (photo ▼).

Playful speed

Travelling with speed and playing with the terrain in chopped-up powder can be a lot of fun. This can mean doing the occasional edge change in the air, which is covered in the Additional Skills chapter. You will feel more confident to travel with speed when your bending and stretching is effective, which can be helped by having the tips level and the skis hip width apart.

Doing an edge change in the air in chopped-up powder (photo ◤).

HEAVY SNOW

This is what light fluffy powder becomes when the temperature increases, or what spring snow can become late in the day when the snow has had lots of sun. In both situations, if you take a handful of the snow, it will feel heavy and makes good snowballs. It can be difficult to spot but you'll know the snow will be heavy if snow is melting on your skis. In the extreme, the snow can become sticky and it will begin to feel like skiing in glue.

Heavy snow on a south-facing slope that has had plenty of sun.

The tracks on the left have been created by a skier who has worked really hard in the heavy snow to push the snow out of the way, seen by the snow displacement to the side of each turn. You could be led to believe this was powder; however, the person who made the tracks on the right can testify that it wasn't!

DIFFERENT TYPES OF SNOW

However the heavy snow has formed, it will be challenging to ski as the skis will be in the snow, and can be likened to trying to ski through a bowl of porridge. Imagine trying to turn skis in porridge, it would be hard work and would require a lot of force.

Speed, spring or snowplough

There are three aids to turning when the snow is really heavy and they are easy to remember as they all start with 'S'. The options are speed, spring, or snowplough, and it is useful to think of them in this order.

Speed

Speed can help in any eventuality where the skis have sunk into the snow. Speed requires confidence and that confidence comes from balancing effectively. A skier becomes good at balancing through having refined the key movements. Skis that are stiff and wide underfoot will also help in these circumstances (but they can be a hindrance in other snow types). Remember that skis cannot be changed halfway down a mountain, but skills can.

Using speed to get through heavy snow. The skier is comfortable with the speed because they are good at balancing, through time spent refining the key movements.

Spring

If the heavy snow is on a slope where you don't feel confident to have lots of speed then another option needs to be chosen. Use a spring to bring the skis towards the surface of the snow, to be able to turn the skis. The spring can be extended further into a jump which is covered in additional skills.

Using a 'spring' to get the skis out of the heavy snow.

OFF-PISTE PERFORMANCE

Snowplough

If it is towards the end of the day, or a ski week, the legs may feel tired, and might not have lots of 'spring' in them. Then there is another option, using a snowplough, or a slight wedge shape. This isn't a defensive action. It is the only practical solution left without the risk of injury. It should be used with confidence and will help build up the experience and skill level to use speed in this situation in the future. Snowploughing is covered in essential skills. By using a snowplough in heavy snow, one of the edges of the skis is placed on an edge before the turn, providing a platform to push the snow out of the way. A snowplough does exactly what it says, it ploughs snow out of the way! There is a gradient where it will feel too steep to snowplough because it becomes strenuous and uncomfortable, but in this situation a side slip will work, as the skis will be on enough of an edge to push the heavy snow down the hill.

The skier has got one of their skis onto its edge early, giving a platform to push the snow out of the way. Snow can be seen being displaced before the turn due to the early edge.

Edge Early – One Ski

Deliberately use a snowplough to start the turn. Do this in slow motion and notice how early it allows the top ski to go onto this new edge, before the turn. This means that there is now something (the base of the ski) which can be used to push the snow out of the way.

Edge early, move snow – both skis

With an understanding of the mechanics of the snowplough, and how having one edge engaged early can help push snow out of the way, let's look at putting two skis on an edge early. This will increase the surface area available to push with; using two bases rather than one. As a reminder, remember that with flat skis it is impossible to move the snow out of the way, making it very difficult to turn when skis are in the snow.

The ski is flat against the surface of the snow, essentially trapped in the snow, with no way of moving the snow out of the way due to the walls on either side.

DIFFERENT TYPES OF SNOW

In this situation, the skier has not engaged either edge until after the skis have passed through the fall line. This works well on a piste but gives no opportunity to push snow out of the way until after the turn, so is not effective when trying to turn skis in heavy snow. This is not a bad habit, just not the right habit for heavy snow.

In this situation the skier has engaged the new edges long before the fall line, giving the opportunity to push snow out of the way with both skis, all the way around the turn.

OFF-PISTE PERFORMANCE

The tracks left after an early edge change, showing that the new edge was engaged before the turn started.

The new edges are engaged before the turn, giving a large platform (both bases) to push heavy snow out of the way. Notice that the skier has not only engaged their edges early but has also started to move to their new 'C' shape before the turn, to balance over the outside ski.

Edge Early – both skis

This drill is excellent for practising engaging both edges as early as possible. Do this on-piste. Build up some speed and then as your skis are travelling across the slope (use a marker pole as a guide), roll the skis onto their new edges prior to going round the corner. It takes an element of commitment and initially it will feel as if you are about to fall over (but you shouldn't!) Imagine you want to show the bases of your skis to the people standing uphill from you, or the top of your skis to people watching from below.

If you do find yourself falling over when you first try this drill, it is most likely because you have tilted the whole body and fallen to the inside of the turn. Remember from Key Movements, balancing over the outside ski, that the upper body will need to tilt in the opposite direction to the edges to remain in balance over the outside ski.

In heavy snow, it is far better to have one ski on its edge early than none, as you can then use it to push the snow out of the way.

DIFFERENT TYPES OF SNOW

A rub-on wax that can be carried in your rucksack.

Wax

In this type of snow, more than any other, wax can play a huge part in how well the skis glide on the surface of the snow. If you know that you are going to be skiing in heavy, potentially sticky, snow then hot wax the skis in advance. It is a good idea to carry a rub-on wax for this eventuality which can be applied out in the field quickly and easily.

As the group have descended the snow quality has deteriorated, both due to altitude and due to timing, and the skiers have found their skis sticking. With a quick coat of wax, the sliding surface improves (photo ◣).

Working the micro aspects

"The weather had been settled for a while with no new snow. The popular Chamonix itineraries accessed by the lift system had all been well skied, with most off-piste tracked out, leaving us with a challenge to find un-skied snow. With good snow becoming scarcer we decided to book a heli-ski drop away from the ski area in Italy.

After a couple of runs warm up in La Thuile, we reached the Petit-Saint-Bernard pass. The helicopter arrived quickly and the pressure was on as the first group got on board and were flown away towards the summits. We were next and once safely airborne the pilot indicated to where the other group were making their descent.

Looking ahead I could see the tell-tale wisps of boot top powder being kicked into the air as the group laid ski tracks in the soft snow. Their line contoured and wrapped around small knolls and micro features.

The party in front was led by an Italian mountain guide, whose chosen line was a master class in working the shady aspects of the slope. It didn't take us long to orientate ourselves and get an idea of where the best snow was – they were "working the micro aspects".

Casually glancing at a map for that area, you could quickly identify East and South-East facing slopes that are exposed to the sun for most of the day. Baked by the sun these slopes were either firm or held breakable crust, the off-piste skier's greatest nemesis. From the map, this did not look like a good choice for off-piste skiing at that time. But due to the small knolls, stream beds, and blunt ridges, there were smaller slopes on the edge of these features that faced North or North-East.

It was these smaller slopes, within a slope, that held cold undisturbed powder that was a joy to ski. We were aided considerably by the previous tracks, but it didn't take long to thread a line that linked these smaller slopes all the way to the valley. The lesson, sometimes you have to work for the best snow available – work the micro aspects."

There is a comprehensive section in Bruce Goodlad's book "*Ski Touring*" on finding good snow.

OFF-PISTE PERFORMANCE

Showing the different strengths of supporting crust. This crust supports the weight of the skier, but not a person travelling on foot.

CRUST

This is frequently a skier's worst nightmare. A crust is formed when weather influences have resulted in a hard layer forming on the surface of the snow, with softer snow underneath. Crusts can vary significantly in strength and may sometimes support the weight of a skier. Other times the skier may break through, often unexpectedly. The skis will be 'on' the snow when skiing supporting crust. Crust that skiers break through is referred to as breakable crust and the skis will be 'in' the snow.

An icy crust that is supporting the weight of a skier (photo ▼).

This looks much like an uphill skinning track, but it's not! It is a downhill track in breakable crust (photo ◤).

Spread the weight

Look back at the example of the person on foot and the person on skis, both standing on the same area of snow. In that instance, the skier has not broken through the crust due to their weight being spread over a larger surface area than the person without skis. To reduce the risk of breaking through the crust, apply this principle to your skiing. Adopt a wider stance and imagine skiing on eggshells, trying not to disturb the snow whilst minimising any sudden movements. In this instance, the weight should be spread more equally over both skis.

Remain focused and alert for the unpredictable breakthrough. When doubtful as to whether the crust is supporting or breakable, it can pay dividends to ski it so as to deliberately break through, then you are dealing with a known quantity, rather than something unpredictable.

DIFFERENT TYPES OF SNOW

Adopting a good stance for a potentially supporting crust (photo ▶).
📷 Bruce Goodlad

The skier has put one ski on an edge early by engaging the big toe on the outside ski. They can then disturb the wind crust that has formed on the surface of the snow and steer the skis effectively. Notice the displaced snow around the boot of the outside ski. At higher speeds, this can be done with both skis at the same time (photo ◀).
📷 Bruce Goodlad

Effortful

Optimum performance in breakable crust takes effort, quite a contrast to the delicate process when trying to remain on a supporting crust. The change in approach required is dramatic. Once in the crust, significant force is required to move the snow out of the way, to allow the skis to turn. Imagine how hard an actual snowplough has to work to move snow. Moving snow in light fluffy powder can be likened to doing a leg press in the gym with very light weights, with which you could do numerous repetitions. Moving snow in heavy snow would be similar to using weights that you could only do a few sets of repetitions with. Moving snow in breakable crust is equivalent to using weights that are near your maximum capability, hence why skiing breakable crust effectively is tiring.

As with heavy snow, the skis need to be on an edge if there is to be any hope of moving the snow. A flat ski will not move snow, and that is why skiing crust on a shallow gradient is one of the hardest things to ski, because the skis are not naturally on an edge. The earlier the skis can be put onto their new edge, the better the position to push the snow out of the way. Remember, it's far better to put one ski on an edge early, than none. Think of engaging the big toe on the outside ski, and then pushing, trying to disturb the snow as much as possible.

When the skis feel truly trapped, such that it's not possible to change the edges in the snow, then using a jump can help. Refer to the section in Additional Skills on jumping, to change the edges of the skis in the air. When applying this jump in crust, it is key to disturb the snow on landing, pushing snow out of the way, to continue the turn. This will only be possible if you land centred on the skis, so pay particular attention to this when practising any jumps, aiming for the whole ski to make contact with the snow at the same time.

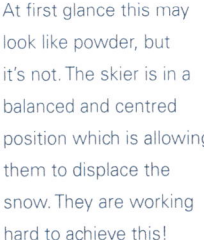

At first glance this may look like powder, but it's not. The skier is in a balanced and centred position which is allowing them to displace the snow. They are working hard to achieve this!

OFF-PISTE PERFORMANCE

> "For the majority of our lesson, I found myself watching Alison from the back and her performance looked effortless. On one descent, in particularly challenging snow, I decided to opt out and skied round on the piste to video the group from below. I then found myself watching Alison descend towards us in the most horrendous breakable crust. Her face said it all. She was trying and working hard. I was surprised by how much effort was going into this seemingly effortless performance. I then tried to replicate an effortful performance rather than an effortless one, and I suddenly found that I had some control over my direction in the breakable crust."

The skis are diverging, making it very difficult for the skier to control their direction in the crusty snow. It's most likely this is happening to the skier in all snow types, but only really becomes problematic when faced with crust.

Perfectly parallel

If there is any divergence in the skis, this will inhibit performance and becomes particularly problematic when skiing crust.

This can be corrected by having an awareness of when the skis are parallel. Put your skis in what you think is a parallel position by looking at the front of the skis. Now, look at the backs. Because of the hourglass shape of skis, when the skis are in fact parallel, it will look like they are in a snowplough shape at the front.

Notice what it feels like in the different positions by trying them with your eyes shut. If you have skied

Skis look parallel at the front but when checking the back of the skis, they are in fact diverging significantly.

Skis are parallel. The skis look like they are in a snowplough when looking at the edges of the skis. Focus on the light blue line down the middle of the skis, indicating that they are parallel.

DIFFERENT TYPES OF SNOW

with the skis diverging for a long time, it will feel like completely different muscles are engaged with the skis in a parallel shape. It can often feel like snowploughing, when in fact you are not.

Sometimes the divergence is caused by an oversteering of the inside foot. Becoming more balanced on the outside ski will help as this will free up the inside ski to be moved as you wish. Try doing the outside ski drills but have an awareness of what the inside ski is doing.

Practice

There is no shortcut to improving skiing in crust. For most people this is the most challenging type of snow to ski, so set realistic expectations. To use an example from mountain biking, it's unlikely that someone will be successful riding a rocky black trail if they have only ever ridden on forest tracks before. In climbing, it is unlikely that someone could climb E7 when only ever having climbed VS. That's what you are asking when skiing breakable crust. It's about the most challenging type of off-piste skiing there is. If there was a quick fix to this, skiers would be doing it, and it wouldn't be challenging. Crust will become easier to ski the better skier you are, so practising all of the key movements repeatedly and in more and more challenging situations will help.

Boots Undone

One of the best advanced drills for skiing in crust is skiing with boots undone, as this helps you to become very good at balancing over the centre of the skis, which is the most efficient and effective place to be for pushing snow out of the way. The key to gaining success from this drill is to do it for long enough that your skiing feels almost 'normal', but travelling at a slightly slower speed, ideally for around half a day.

Completely undo your ski boots. If they are touring boots, then leave them in ski mode. Select a quiet piste with a gentle gradient and good firm snow to get used to the feeling. Feel that you need to press down through your heel to remain in balance, with your shin in contact with the front of the boot. You will know that you are doing it right if you don't fall over, have control over where you are going, and over your speed. Progress to more challenging piste terrain, and then to off-piste terrain. Try doing many of the other drills in this book with your boots undone.

By the end of the practice session, you should feel more connected to your skis than you have ever been. Boots that fit well are great for being responsive, but they can also let you get away with being slightly out of balance, without knowing it, and wondering why crust is always so difficult.

Undoing boots completely for a morning's skiing.

OFF-PISTE PERFORMANCE

> Trying to twist skis in heavy snow or breakable crust is one of the main causes of skiing knee injuries. This is often done when trying to force a parallel turn when initiating the turn with a snowplough would have been more appropriate, because of the early edge and pushing potential this gives. The injury is frequently blamed on a binding not releasing, whereas in fact the injury occurred at the twisting stage, before the fall and point of release. Use a snowplough to initiate the turn in these snow types to avoid this happening.

There are two types of snow worth recognising, neither being a favourable skiing surface. They are mentioned here so that they can be avoided.

Rain Runnels

A unique set of circumstances lead to these being formed. They occur when heavy rain falls onto dry cold snow, causing the rain to flow down the hill in channels, forming runnels running parallel to the fall line of the slope. Frequently a crust forms on the surface, if there is subsequently a drop in temperature. Thankfully these are quite rare, although as we experience bigger fluctuations in temperature during winter they are becoming increasingly common. The surface becomes an icy, breakable crust, The runnels will appear on all slopes, irrespective of aspect, at the altitudes where it was raining. If it's not possible to ski above where it rained, then it is a day for skiing on the piste. However, these can become fun to ski when, and if, the surface of the runnels starts to soften.

Sastrugi

Sections of sastrugi most frequently occur on large, open flat areas where the wind can be at its strongest. Sastrugi looks much like waves, with the points facing into the wind. They can be over 1m high! Thankfully this normally doesn't coincide with favourable off-piste terrain as it is often easy angled or flat, so it may just be a case of 'getting across it'. Do not try to go too fast as the tips of the skis can dig into a drift and stop, with the skier going over the front of the skis.

Rain runnels and sastrugi, best avoided if at all possible.

TERRAIN VARIATIONS

The skier is currently enjoying an easy angled wide-open space, but is mentally preparing for steeper slopes beneath the convexity, which the skier can't currently see.

Groomed slopes tend to follow the natural fall line of the mountain and avoid dips and gullies which may be challenging to the skier. Also, the ground surface is sometimes landscaped in the summer months, resulting in a smooth and uniform slope to ski on. In contrast, no such management is done off-piste, with the snow falling onto an unprepared surface. An off-piste skier needs to be able to adapt their skills to deal with whatever terrain is encountered. There are many potential variations, but they will mostly fall into one of the categories that follow. Each category is looked at in isolation, showing how skiing skills can be adapted to fit whatever terrain changes you are faced with. However, within one off-piste descent, many of these terrain features will come in quick succession, highlighting how versatile and adaptable the off-piste skill set needs to be.

For example, imagine the following descent. The run may start as a wide-open snowfield, and then the slope disappears in front of you over a convexity, giving uncertainty as to what comes next. On approach, you discover that the steepening slope is channelled into a narrow gully. At the exit of the gully, you arrive at the treeline and have to ski between closely spaced trees. Then you pick up a narrow path to take you back to the lifts.

Within this one descent, lots of variations are required to maintain a feeling of flow and rhythm. By reading the description above, you have already undertaken one of the key practices, which is to visualise what you might expect to happen over the whole run. Depending on how the off-piste descent is accessed, there may be opportunities to use the uphill travel time to prepare for the downhill. While riding the chairlift, or skinning uphill, have a look at what is to come. Visualise yourself making changes, adapting to the terrain in front of you. The changes will appear fast when skiing, so visualising the changes in advance allows the run to be rehearsed in slow motion.

STEEP

Rather than put a defined gradient on what is described as steep, think of steep as anything that makes your heart rate increase because of the gradient in front of you. This will be different for everyone, and may mean something different to the same person, on the same slope, but on another day. A slope might not feel steep when it is covered in fresh powder, but come back another day when it is icy and it will feel completely different, perhaps feeling steep when previously it did not. The same skill set needs to be deployed when a slope 'feels' steep, rather than necessarily is steep. For most skiers, this means keeping the speed down, maintaining a feeling of control and knowing that you are turning the skis when and where you want to.

> *"The basic principle is keeping your speed down. The risk of falling is much greater on steep slopes, so it is extremely important to keep your speed to an absolute minimum when initiating a turn."*
> Anselme Baud 2002 (IFMGA Mountain Guide and pioneering extreme skier)

Working with this principle, the skis need to be turned without gathering much, or any, speed. Therefore, twisting the skis is fundamental to success on steeper terrain. If the skis are turned in a small space, you will gather less speed. Hence there are huge similarities between techniques for steep terrain and for narrow terrain, and often what is steep is also narrow. The key to success is practising these turns before they are required, and that requires significant discipline and motivation.

'Steep' can mean different things to different people.

TERRAIN VARIATIONS

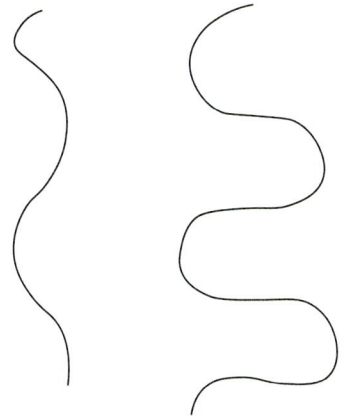

The skis are not coming perpendicular to the fall line on the line on the left, but they are on the right. Spend time practising skiing the line on the right to ensure you are good at balancing through the end of the turn.

Practice perpendicular

One of the first things that will occur when faced with steep terrain, is that skiers bring the skis perpendicular to the slope at the end of the turn, to control speed. This is a good thing to do, and an effective way to control speed. However, it is less common that skiers ski this sort of line when on terrain that isn't steep, as it takes much longer to get from A to B. Therefore, skiers are less familiar with the body movements required to stay in balance at the end of the turn when the skis come perpendicular to the slope and can find themselves out of balance at this point. Spend time practising skiing a line where the skis come perpendicular to the slope as part of your training. Try some of the drills in this book skiing the same line.

Pole plant position

Pole plant position is crucial on steeper ground. Stand with your skis perpendicular to the slope. Reach behind to plant the pole near the back of your bindings, opening out the shoulder joint. This turns your body to face downhill, gives space for your skis to turn, and allows space for the movement of bringing your hips in front of the feet. Notice that the skis will start to twist of their own accord if the pole plant is in this place. It's worth contrasting this with the counter movement of pole planting near the front of your skis. Notice how this turns your body into the slope, blocks the possibility of moving the hip forward and does not contribute to getting the skis to turn.

This pole plant is hindering performance in steep terrain. The pole plant is blocking the key movement of moving the hips forward, blocking where the skis need to turn and has turned the body to face up the hill.

This pole plant is helpful to performance in steep terrain. The skis have space to turn in a small area. The body has been turned towards the fall line. The hips can move freely in front of the feet.

OFF-PISTE PERFORMANCE

Ensure the pole plant position helps, rather than hinders the performance. The great thing about the pole position is that this can be thought of when stationary in preparation for the turn, giving time to experiment with different positions and understand their implications.

💡 "I used to traverse a steep slope, reach forward to near the tips of my skis, pole plant determined to turn, and then decide not to turn. I thought the pole plant would help me to commit to the turn, but it didn't. I would repeat this a few times before I found myself at the edge of the steep slope, on the steepest part, and still not able to execute a turn. I changed where I pole planted to behind me, and then I found that my pole plant helped me commit to the turn as the skis started to turn when I pole planted. I now think of pole planting 'forward' as pole planting down the slope behind me, rather than near the front of my skis."

Body momentum

The key movement of moving forward into the turn is critical to success on steeper terrain. It ensures that the skis can be turned quickly and easily from the fall line to across the slope, as it's the moment when the skis are in the fall line that most speed will be gathered. The steeper it is, the faster and more dynamic the movement forward into the turn needs to be. The body should have lots of momentum, and the skis little momentum. Try doing an extra little sink down before bringing the hips across the skis, as this makes the movement more dynamic.

'C' shape, 'C' shape, 'C' shape

'C' shape is essential to being balanced over the outside (lower) ski at the end of the turn and staying in control. As shown earlier in the book there are a number of ways to maintain 'C' shape. On steeper terrain aim to have a trigger word that helps you to exaggerate this position. Here are some suggested ones.

- Top hand high
- Bottom hand low
- Squeeze (rib cage and hip bone together on downhill side)
- Stretch (on uphill side)
- Tilt

Maintaining good balance over the outside (lower) ski at the end of the turn on steep terrain. Have a trigger word to help you to achieve this.

TERRAIN VARIATIONS

This is a highly proficient skier who is getting into their 'C' shape position really early in the turn, so that they will already be in it by the time the skis come perpendicular to the slope.

Skis on the snow

The skis should be kept on the snow, if at all possible, while twisting them. At first this can feel hard, and the instinct may be to jump, but with pole planting behind and developing twisting skills, this will be the most efficient way to turn in a small space, or on steep ground. Jumping requires a lot more effort and accuracy, and puts a greater load on the slope and body. If the skis are 'on' the snow rather than in it, take full advantage of these conditions and aim to twist the skis on the surface.

Turn in a Box

This is a great drill for practising turning in a small space without gathering much speed. It is rarely done enough and is excellent for gaining confidence for steeper terrain. Draw a small box and try to turn your skis without coming out of the box, either at the sides or the bottom. Try turning the skis in the space with a jump. Notice the effort that is required to do this. Now try doing the same but keeping the skis on the snow. Keeping the skis on the snow will feel far less tiring, and will therefore be easier to replicate turn after turn down a long slope. It does take practice though!

Exercise of turning in a box, which is excellent to gain confidence for turning in a small space and is helpful for both steep and narrow terrain.

OFF-PISTE PERFORMANCE

Lots of Turns

Practise these turns on a slope where it doesn't 'feel' steep. People rarely do this as nobody would want to ski with them, as you'll do a lot of turns but not cover much ground. Pick two piste markers, and imagine a line down the side of the piste. Try and get as many turns as you can into this narrow corridor. Do this again and try and increase the number. Check that the speed isn't getting faster and faster as this will come with consequences when transferred to steeper terrain.

Aiming to get as many turns as possible in between the two yellow and black marker poles (photo ▶).

Those competing in the Freeride World Tour may not agree with Anselme Baud's statement regarding keeping the speed down, and of course steep slopes can be skied at speed. This shows one of the great things about off-piste skiing. The sport is incredibly diverse. People can be successful skiing down steep slopes both fast and slow. There is not only one way to do it. If skiing steep slopes fast, bending and stretching is of great importance. The legs need to be flexed ready to absorb whatever comes in the path. Balancing over the outside ski is fundamental whether skiing steeps fast or slow.

The skiers here have taken a fast line down the steep slope, doing very few turns.

Steep skiing

The term 'extreme skiing' was first heard around the late 1960s when the likes of Sylvain Saudan, Patrick Vallencant, Anselme Baud, Jean-Marc Boivin and Bruno Gouvy started to ski steeper lines around the Mont Blanc Massif. These lines seemed impossible to the recreational skier, taking the limits of the sport into a new era. The first World Ski Extreme Championships in Alaska in 1991, won by Doug Combs and Kim Reichhelm, evolved into the Freeride World Tour which, in 2004, brought skiers and snowboarders together for the first time competing on the world's steepest faces, taking in cliff jumps, narrow couloirs and everything in between.

The way in which steep slopes are skied has changed dramatically over the last few decades, as has the equipment. In the 1991 championships there were no helmets, no rucksacks, and no back protectors,

TERRAIN VARIATIONS

all of which are mandatory in today's Freeride World Tour, along with airbags, transceivers, shovels and probes. In 1991 the skiers were doing more turns and fewer cliff jumps. Today the skiers take straighter lines and incorporate cliff drops and tricks into their runs. Athletes are judged on the complexity of their line, how much control they have, the fluidity of their performance, air time, style and their overall technique. Through the decades the key movements have stayed the same. The skiers are all good at balancing over the outside ski, bending and stretching, and moving forward into the turn. They are also using a combination of twisting and edging when they turn, blended according to the terrain and snow type. They all use the essential skills of side slipping and traversing to make progress down the mountain.

Freerider Amy Marwick on steep terrain (photo ▼).
📷 George McIlenan

Freeride skier taking a fast line with few turns down a steep slope (photo ▶).
📷 George McIlenan

Personal reflection

In 2011 I decided to book some off-piste skiing with French IFMGA Mountain Guide Rémy Lécluse. This was so that I could tackle some steep slopes that I did not want to ski by myself. When I first met Rémy he made it very clear that if he was going to guide me on steep slopes, I had to ski his way or he wouldn't ski with me.

Our first ski together was to be a 'warm up' day to practise his way of skiing. A quick non-stop lap off the top bin at Les Grands Montets and he had enough time to make an assessment of me. While he was checking out conditions through his binoculars, I was catching my breath. He asked me if I used to race, "Yes" I replied proudly, pleased that he had observed that in my skiing so quickly. "And how many times did you crash in races?" I replied it was probably about 1 in 7. "When you ski these types of slopes with me you can never crash. It's not an option." The message was clear.

We stood at the top of the face and he said "Right, I want to see you do 5 turns between here and there without jump turning". I looked at him blankly, "Without jumping?" "Yes" he replied, "You need to keep your skis on the snow". The learning began. He explained that jumping was a high-risk manoeuvre and steep slopes were not a place to do it. The same result could be achieved by keeping the skis on the snow the majority of the time.

He spoke to me sternly when I forgot to stop above him. Sternly in a reassuring way; I was reassured that he was giving me 100% of his attention and that my safety was his main focus. After the couloir, we had a warm down run where I was following him back through the forest. He was doing hundreds of quick turns in quick succession down the track and I was cruising behind. He stopped and shouted, "Do you think I'm doing all these turns for my benefit?" I guess not. I followed behind, trying to copy him, doing more turns than I would ever have done down this slope.

With the warm up day over, I was delighted with what we had achieved and what I had learnt, and we still had the "adventure" day to come. Rémy had some ideas of where we might go but nothing was set in stone. His flexible approach demonstrated that he was responding to the conditions in front of him. Bring everything, and be prepared to go anywhere. It wasn't until we skied down onto the Argentière Glacier that he made a firm decision. "Let's go for the South West Couloir on the Chardonnet." "Where?" He explained. I looked at my watch. We are going to go from here to the top of the Chardonnet, today? I'm glad he's breaking trail. The conditions were perfect for skiing downhill; fresh untracked powder everywhere with little effect from the wind or sun. But it certainly made it hard work to go uphill; I was crawling uphill behind him. I didn't take a camera. I tend not to when I need to focus. But the memories of the descent are still vivid in my mind. There was beautiful fresh powder all the way through the couloirs that twist between the huge red granite towers. Rómy danced down effortlessly, demonstrating exactly how he wanted me to ski. I tried to replicate it and I would hear his voice reminding me when I didn't, "Don't jump. Keep your skis on the snow", "Double pole plant". He could fit turns in where I aspired to. Eventually, we skied out the bottom of the couloir. I don't remember many stops between there and the Pierre à Ric Piste. We skied down the piste amongst the skiers that we had begun the day with. Glancing back up at the Chardonnet, I felt quietly privileged that our day had probably been quite different to theirs. All thanks to Rémy.

Rémy was renowned for his own personal achievements, but he also had a unique skill in guiding people in this environment too, teaching them and helping people to accomplish their goals. He was 'the Godfather' of steep skiing in every way. I'll continue to aspire to dance down ski slopes with the fluidity that he did and to coach others to do the same. Rémy Lécluse is the greatest loss to skiing I have ever known.

Rémy Lécluse was tragically killed in an avalanche on Manaslu in September 2012.

IFMGA Mountain Guide Rémy Lécluse.
📷 Alan Scowcroft

TERRAIN VARIATIONS

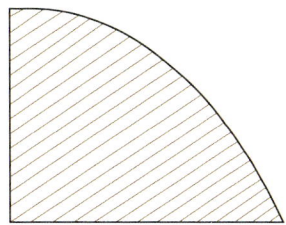

CONVEX

A convex slope is one that starts off gently and becomes progressively steeper while descending. On a convex slope, the skier will be unable to have a complete view of the slope they are about to ski.

A side-on profile of a convex slope.

The skier is stood on the convexity, having gone to look at the slope beneath him.

A convex slope. The skier does not have a full view of the slope that they are descending. They can just see the two heads of the rest of their team, but they cannot see the slope between themselves and the team.

Prepare for steepness

The main challenge with a convex slope is not being able to see what comes next. However, when you notice that a slope is disappearing in front of you, you do know what comes next. The slope is going to get steeper. This is what you need to prepare for. Focus on the movements that will be required for the increase in gradient, rather than on what you cannot see.

You can prepare for this by making your turns more twisty and getting ready to move forward more into the turn. As the gradient steepens, the

OFF-PISTE PERFORMANCE

likelihood is that the skis will come further across the fall line (perpendicular) and this means that balance needs to be maintained over the outside ski. As a result, you will need more 'C' shape with the body. Start exaggerating these movements before they are required. Then, when the slope ahead comes into view you will be ready and prepared. If it turns out not to be as steep as expected, that is fine, it's better to be over-prepared than under-prepared. If obstacles appear that need avoiding, you will be in a good position on the skis to control your speed and stop if required.

"I used to find myself out of balance on my first turn as I came over a rise and the skis would shoot ahead of me. I would have travelled halfway across the slope before I was able to even contemplate doing the next turn. By having my top hand high, my balance came over my outside (lower) ski and I had much more control. Now, as I see a rise coming, I put my uphill hand high in preparation, as if I am waving at someone uphill of me. It feels slightly daft, as it's exaggerated for the gentle slope that I am on, but it means I am prepared for the steeper slope ahead and looks less daft than shooting across the hill out of control."

Preparing for going onto a steeper slope by getting their uphill hand high in advance of being on the slope.

This line varies the turn shape and size of the turns and as a result speed will also change, which replicates the adjustments that will be needed off-piste for terrain changes.

Vary the Turns

Practise varying the turns, both in speed and size. Set off doing fast, wide turns where using the edge to turn is the primary movement. Do about five or six turns. Then reduce the speed and the size of the turn to twisty turns in a narrow corridor. Do about five or six turns. Then increase the speed and size of turn again. Repeat. Notice the length and width of the space required to go from big, fast turns to small, narrow turns. This drill is excellent for dealing with terrain changes. If the turn can't be adapted and changed on a smooth piste, then it's not going to happen off-piste.

TERRAIN VARIATIONS

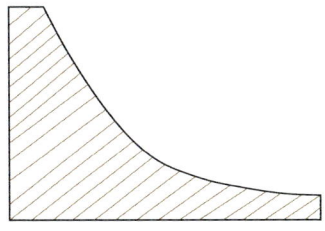

CONCAVE

A concave slope is one which becomes progressively less steep while descending. Typically, a slope will be convex at the top and concave at the bottom.

A side-on profile of a concave slope.

The skier is on a concave slope and has a clear view of the slope below, where the gradient eases (photo ▲).

Not only is there a change in gradient but there is also a change in snow type, due to the steeper slope being in the shade and the flatter area being in the sun (photo ◤).

Prepare for the flat

All too often skiers successfully negotiate a challenging section and then fall or lose balance on the flat section at the bottom. Due to the sudden change in angle, the terrain change is often coupled with a change in snow type, usually a less favourable one. You can ski a nice powder field and then find the flatter snow at the bottom is crusty due to having had more sun.

When transitioning to the flat, anticipate the change, remain engaged and stay alert, as this can be the crux. Keep the core engaged and be in a strong position to deal with the changes. Don't ease off.

Recognise if the skis are in or on the snow. If the skis are in the snow, you will need to have them on an edge to push the snow out of the way. If twisty turns were used on the steeper section, these are likely to be less effective on the flatter section, so carry some speed onto the flat, so that edging can be used successfully.

As the gradient eases, the likelihood is that the skis will take a more direct line and this means that the balance will become more equal across the two skis.

"Rather embarrassingly, after having successfully negotiated the steep section that I had been so worried about, I fell on the flat slope at the bottom, right in front of the rest of the group. I had relaxed and stopped doing all the good movements that I had been doing down the steep section. Now I always stay focused and alert as I come on to the easier ground."

OFF-PISTE PERFORMANCE

The convexities have less snow cover with rocks and grass exposed (photo ▼).

The gully centre has deeper snow than the gully sides (photo ▶).

Convexities can have thinner snow cover due to the wind stripping the snow away from this point, so be alert for more rocks showing through in this area. Conversely, concave areas will have more snow build up so be prepared for deeper snow in these locations, the skis might change from being on the surface to being in the snow.

The same thing can occur in gullies. There will be more snow build up in the centre and more rocks at the edge, so ski the sides with caution.

BUMPS

Bumps, or moguls, form where the snow has been pushed together by lots of skiers skiing similar lines. This is most frequently found off-piste where skiers are channelled to follow the same route, for example, because of trees, cliffs, or glacial features. A classic example of this is in Chamonix on the Vallée Blanche, where skiers pass through the Géant Icefall, which is notorious for becoming bumpy when it hasn't snowed for a long time.

Bumps and troughs can also be present on the bed surface, underneath the snow, but the way in which the ski skills need to be adapted is the same.

Les Grands Montets, Chamonix, can become one large bump field when there hasn't been fresh snow for a while.

TERRAIN VARIATIONS

Bumps on the Vallée Blanche, beside the Géant Icefall.

Options rather than limits

It's easy to feel limited as to where to turn when faced with bumps. Instead, see options. Where bumps exist, the surface area to ski on is far greater than if the same area didn't have bumps. As an illustration, visualise lying a blanket over a slope with bumps on, with the blanket touching all of the peaks and troughs of every bump. Remove the blanket from the bumps and stretch it out. The blanket will extend way beyond the boundaries of the bump field.

The increased surface area presents the skier with more options. There are more places to turn and there are more places to control speed. The great thing about bumps is that they can be skied successfully in a number of different ways, so there is not just one line that can be taken through them, but endless possibilities.

See options, not limitations.

OFF-PISTE PERFORMANCE

These skiers are on the smallest of bumps, but it is enough to make the skis easy to twist, as the tips and tails are free to move because they are off the surface of the snow. You will start to see bumps on the smoothest slopes.

Skiing a fast line through the bumps, staying mainly in the troughs.

Tops for twist, troughs for speed

Aim for the tops of the bumps if you wish to ski slowly. Think back to the turning options. It will be very difficult to do a twisty turn with the skis in the trough, as the tips and tails of the skis will get caught as they are rotated. The skis will be much easier to pivot if they are on a bump, as the tips and tails are free to rotate.

Skiing the troughs can be fun and fast, but be alert and ready to use a bump to control your speed. Skiing the troughs is much like the line you could imagine a bobsleigh taking through the bumps. If you ski the bumps fast, the bending and stretching movement will need to be used through its full range to stay in balance.

TERRAIN VARIATIONS

Aim for a high point
Just as is instinctive when walking, aim for a high point, as you can get a view of what is coming next and make a decision about the next part of the route. You can also identify places to control speed.

This skier has just twisted the skis on a high point and is now entering into a side slip down the back side of the bump. They will then cross the trough, using the trough wall as a cushion to help control their speed.

The gradients vary considerably within a field of bumps. Here the skier is on a micro steep slope within an easy-angled bumpy area and has adjusted their body position to stay balanced over the outside (lower) ski and maintain control.

Is it steep or flat?
Consider the gradient within the bumps, rather than the gradient of the whole slope. For example, you might be on a 20 degree slope, but within it, because of the bumps, some areas are much steeper and some areas are much flatter. The body position needs to be constantly adjusted to the micro changes in gradient.

If the skis are travelling over a shallow gradient, then you will be balanced more equally over both skis, but when on a steep section you will need to adapt and change to balance over the outside ski. It can be challenging to balance if one ski is on steep terrain whilst the other is on flatter ground. Therefore, aim to adopt a width of stance which allows both skis to travel over a similar gradient at the same time. Often, this will be around hip width apart.

133

OFF-PISTE PERFORMANCE

Point the toes
When descending into a trough, point the toes down into the trough to gain maximum ski-to-snow contact, rather than feel like you are 'plopping' off the bump. This will mean stretching the legs as you point the toes down into the trough, and then letting the legs retract underneath you coming up the next bump, ready to stretch again.

The skier is pointing their toes to keep the front of the ski in contact with the snow.

NARROW

As with steep terrain, think of narrow as any terrain that feels narrow, rather than applying a fixed width. In theory, you should be able to turn your skis in an area matching the length of the skis. In order to turn in a narrow space, twisting needs to be used. This can be done with the skis on the snow, or with them in the air, which is covered in the Additional Skills chapter.

Skiers faced with various types of narrow terrain.

TERRAIN VARIATIONS

Skiers faced with various types of narrow terrain.

The skier is using a pole plant near the back of their binding to help initiate the turn in a narrow place.

Pole plant

As with skiing on steep terrain, pole planting behind the feet near the back of the binding will help considerably. This will give space for the skis to turn and rotate the upper body down the hill, leaving only the lower body and skis to be turned.

Twist from the centre of the foot

To turn in the smallest area possible, you will need to twist from the centre of the foot. Twist around the front of the skis, and the turning area will be double the length of the skis. Twist around the tails of the skis, and the turning area will also be double the length of the skis, and will also be tiresome. Twist from the centre of the foot, and the skis can turn in an area no greater than the length of the ski. Imagine a rod through the body, this is where the pivot point needs to be.

OFF-PISTE PERFORMANCE

The line indicates where you are aiming for the tips of the skis to travel. If done proficiently, the ski tips will not cross the line.

Central Twist

This is a great drill to practise twisting from the centre of the foot. Stand perpendicular to the slope. Mark a line going from the tips of your skis to the fall line. This will be a quarter circle. Aim to turn without the tips of the skis crossing the line at any point.

Psychological practice

Often the greatest challenge associated with narrow terrain is the psychological barrier it presents and this needs to be trained for.

Barriers

Draw some lines in the snow and try to turn within these boundaries. This can be achieved off-piste with two skiers leaving a narrow corridor in the middle, in which you will aim to do your turns. Return to the central twist drill and have a person right beside you, to restrict any forward movement. They provide a barrier, but one which can move out of the way if required! The same thing can be done with the person standing beneath you, but this requires care and attention. The person needs to be positioned to side slip out of the way quickly if they can see that your turn isn't going to fit into the gap.

Aim to have your tracks in the space indicated.

TERRAIN VARIATIONS

Keeping the feet on the highest point, to have the tips and tails of the skis light, to aid speed control.

Negotiating a narrow gully (photo ▼).

The bow effect when in a trough or gully, making it difficult to twist the skis (photo ◀).

Ridges and Gullies

There are two main opposing features within the narrow category. There are narrow ridges and narrow gullies.

Narrow ridge

Normally in mountain terms, a ridge is thought of on a large scale, like a ridge running down from the top of a mountain. In this instance, think of a ridge on a small scale, a feature where the slope drops away on both the left and right of your skis. On such a ridge line, the tips and tails of the skis will be lighter, sometimes in the air. This makes using a twisty turn the favoured choice if a change of direction is required. Alternatively, the skier may choose to side slip down the line of the ridge, keeping their feet on the highest point of the ridge, to have the greatest speed control, as shown in the traversing chapter.

Narrow gully

This describes a narrow section where the terrain goes up on either side, most commonly when natural dips or river beds fill in with snow. Half pipes are manmade gullies. Twisting can be difficult because of the bow effect of the skis.

The base of the ski may not be touching the snow, making a pure twist movement challenging. In this case, it's better to use some speed or move to a different place. Using a bit of speed to go up the side of gullies can be great fun, and also assist the turn.

OFF-PISTE PERFORMANCE

The tiniest of bumps will make it easier to twist the skis (photo ▲).

This skier is finding ridges within a gully to assist with twisting the skis (photo ◤).

When faced with a turn in a narrow gully and you'd like to ski slowly or slow down, search out even the tiniest of bumps as it will make it easier to twist the skis. You will start finding bumps where you have never seen bumps before! If you want to twist the skis, move to a place where it's possible to twist them freely.

TREES

Skiing off-piste in perfectly spaced trees can bring immense pleasure, moving freely from one turn to the next, the turn size being dictated by the variable gaps between the trees. Equally, this experience can be intimidating, particularly when faced with it for the first time. Skiing through trees can be imagined as a magical experience with fresh cold powder everywhere, with the snow still hanging on the tree branches. While this is sometimes the reality, it can also mean skiing through trees with any of the snow types mentioned in the previous chapter, which can result in much more challenging experiences.

Tree skiing in dense forest with small gaps.

TERRAIN VARIATIONS

Tree skiing amongst small birch trees provides some definition on a poor visibility day (photo ▲).

Skiing chopped-up powder in some larger spaces within the trees (photo ◤).

What's under the surface?

One of the main challenges with tree skiing in fresh powder is knowing what is underneath the surface. Gaining some knowledge of this is helpful to either have increased confidence when skiing the trees, or know that these trees are best to be avoided. Knowing the history of the previous snowfalls will be helpful. For example, is this the first snowfall of the season? If so, there is likely to be no base and the tree skiing will be poor. Was there a firm base in existence before the snowfall? If yes, then the tree skiing is more likely to be good. Also, look at the base of the trees and observe how well buried they are.

Look for an appropriate line through the trees, whether this be tightly spaced trees or ones with wider gaps. If skinning or riding the chairlift, try and spot the entry point and line on the way up, and look at it from the angle you will approach from.

Preparation for skiing trees by taking hands out of pole straps.

! Take your hands out of the straps on your poles. If the baskets of the poles get caught in the trees or undergrowth, you want the pole to come out of your hand to avoid a shoulder injury.

Go first

Frequently the most confident skiers will go first, racing to get fresh tracks through the trees, getting plenty of resistance to control their speed from the freshly fallen snow. The weaker skiers hold back, finding little fresh powder for resistance and then accelerating in places where those in front were slowing down, resulting in a very different experience, requiring different skills. The powder between the trees gives resistance to slow the skis down, take full advantage of this and go first.

OFF-PISTE PERFORMANCE

There is still plenty of space to get fresh tracks in this photo. The skier is eyeing up the untracked snow ahead of them as the preferred line (photo ▼).

Aim for the untracked
Given that not everybody can go first, the next strategy is to look for fresh snow to help with speed control. Naturally, the first people through the trees will go an equal distance between two trees, meaning that the remaining fresh snow is closer to the trees. Aim for the fresh snow as it gives an opportunity to control speed rather than hurtling through the middle.

Skier looking ahead in the trees (photo ◤).

Read the snow, not the trees
Look ahead at the snow and anticipate the line. Do not look at the trees, or you will find your skis heading towards them. Instead, focus your attention on the line between the trees and on reading the terrain.

💡 When I heard 'tree skiing' referred to as 'gap skiing' and started to focus on the gaps when skiing the trees, I could feel a noticeable improvement in my performance. Prior to this, even the mention of the phrase 'tree skiing' would bring tension into my body, and this would escalate upon seeing the trees. Now I focus on calling this skiing 'gap skiing' and then I see the gaps, focus on the gaps, and ski through the gaps, in a relaxed and rhythmical way with a smile on my face.

Attention is fully focused on the gaps.

TERRAIN VARIATIONS

PATHS

Most commonly, skiers encounter paths at the bottom of a run, when skiing on tired legs. Paths can have all different types of terrain within them: ridges, bumps, gullies, tight corners, the odd rock or tree root pointing through with the added challenge of a human traffic jam thrown in. They are mostly narrow, flat, and follow the line of a summer footpath. It's good to learn to ski paths efficiently as they are often a place where injuries occur due to tiredness at the end of the day's skiing.

All the challenges of narrow paths.

Move snow, scrub speed

Speed can be scrubbed by an active movement of the skis sideways. Remember the action when the skis are 'in' the snow, of pushing the snow out of the way. This is the same action, only that the skis may be on the snow rather than in it. As a result, more force is needed to push into and move the snow surface. Scrub is the key word, as that is exactly what it feels like. It isn't coming to a stop; it is dumping a bit of speed. In this case, the skis don't come perpendicular to the path, but rather stay much more direct. On many paths there isn't space for the skis to come perpendicular to the path. If the skis do come perpendicular to the path, the skier would most likely stop and others could crash into the back of them.

Practising scrubbing speed on a narrow section on-piste. The 'scrub' is shown by the snow being displaced.

OFF-PISTE PERFORMANCE

Take opportunities to control speed. In this photo, a bit of speed can be scrubbed by pushing into softer snow on the left hand side, before the approaching corner.

Opportunities for speed control

Identify opportunities to control your speed and take them. For example, it's going to be really hard to control speed in a channel down the middle of the path. However, move the feet to the ridge at the edge and it might be possible to side slip to scrub off a bit of speed. There might be patches of untracked snow, which will give resistance and slow the speed.

Little and often

It takes time and space to slow down from a fast speed, and time and space are not always plentiful on these types of tracks. Therefore, it is much better to scrub off a little bit of speed frequently, rather than finding yourself having to drastically reduce speed quickly. Even if a reduction in speed is not required at that point in time, when you see an opportunity to scrub speed take it, as you don't know when the next opportunity will arise.

COMBINING SNOW AND TERRAIN VARIATIONS

Combining skills to match the prevailing snow conditions and the terrain.

Having looked at the different snow and terrain types which may be encountered when skiing off-piste, it becomes evident just how many possible combinations there are and how diverse the off-piste skier's skill set needs to be, to ski all of these well. For example, steep terrain could be met with any of the snow types on it, anything from the lightest of powder to the firmest snow, and any of the possibilities in between. Similarly, a narrow section could have grippy, hard-packed snow in it and be skied like a piste. Equally it could be covered in breakable crust. That's why it is important to become skilful with all of the movements so that they can be applied in different ways, at different times, to achieve different outcomes.

There are challenges in combining the movements and strategies for varying snow and different terrain, as they may seem to contradict each other. This is when skiing can become particularly challenging, but even more satisfying when mastered skilfully. Let's look at three exceptionally challenging combinations. With a little knowledge of the key movements and ways of turning, they are not as complex as they may first appear.

How do you ski powder on steep terrain?

On terrain that you feel is 'steep' the first inclination is to think of doing twisty turns as this means there will be less speed gathered. However, you know that twisty turns don't work effectively when the skis are 'in' the snow.

OFF-PISTE PERFORMANCE

Skier achieving success on a steep slope on a powder day, by using the resistance of the snow to control the speed, and turning the tips of the skis slightly uphill at the end of the turn to control speed further if needed.

In this case, the powder snow will give the resistance to keep the speed manageable, so an edgy turn can work. The mountain can also be used to slow the speed, by turning the skis further uphill at the end of the turn. Remember that skis can be turned beyond perpendicular to the mountain and point uphill (refer to diagram 'Practice Perpendicular' in the section on Steep Terrain). Finding the 'sweet spot' is important, so that the speed is slowed enough to feel comfortable, but not stalled so that the fronts of the skis dive into the powder.

How do you ski powder in narrow terrain?

In narrow places, snow will only be powder for the passage of a few skiers. If you are skiing in a group, the person at the front will be faced with a very different situation to the person at the back. The first person may have used a 'spring' to get their skis to the surface of the snow, whereas the person that comes last might find that their skis are on the surface, and a twisting action on the ground works effectively. If the snow is heavy, a jump turn might be needed to get the skis out of the snow. These are described in Additional Skills.

The first skiers down this section skied powder, but this skier is faced with a different situation. All of the fresh powder has been scraped off, leaving firm, hard-packed snow where the skis are on the surface of the snow.

COMBINING SNOW AND TERRAIN VARIATIONS

Here the skier is in a narrow couloir. However, due to the right-hand section of the gully being in the sun, the snow there is poor. The skier is opting to stay in the shaded area which still has cold powder snow, making the gully even narrower than it looks.

How do you ski crust in a narrow gully?
Because a gully has different aspects, it would be particularly unlucky to find crust all around the gully. This is only likely if the crust has been caused by rain, rather than sun or wind. It might be that the snow is slightly better on one side and a tactical decision is taken to stay on one side of the gully. If there is crust all around the gully, then this is another place where jump turns may be required as there might not be enough space to place the skis on edge early.

POOR VISIBILITY

Skiers being challenged by the poor visibility, where it is difficult to see the terrain or snow type clearly. These skiers have chosen to ski near some marker poles which provide some definition (photo ▲).

Following infrastructure such as a snow fence can be helpful in poor visibility (photo ◄).

The only thing these skiers have to provide some definition is other skiers (photo ►).

It's a powder day, but it is challenging to enjoy as the light is flat so it's impossible to judge the gradient of the slope (photo far ►).

As you develop an understanding of all the potential variations of types of snow and terrain, there is one other major factor which adds to the complexity of off-piste skiing. It doesn't fit neatly into the chapter on types of snow or the chapter on terrain variations, but it has a major influence on performance. That is skiing in poor visibility and flat light.

Skiing in poor visibility is challenging and can be unpleasant. It is a problem mostly associated with bad weather, but vision can become impaired on an overcast day when the definition of the slope is lost, referred to as skiing in 'flat light'. Skiing in poor visibility is less of a problem when skiing on piste as the

OFF-PISTE PERFORMANCE

Appropriate goggles are hugely beneficial in poor visibility.

marker poles at the edge of the run provide some definition, and there is an element of reassurance about the terrain in that the slope has been checked by ski patrol. Off-piste, poor visibility can result in all definition being lost; therefore, knowledge of the terrain and snow type can be severely restricted.

In the majority of circumstances, it is better to avoid skiing off-piste in these conditions because of the hazard this presents, particularly if you are prone to feeling sick in such conditions. However, you may find that you get caught out in such conditions, so it is good to have a few coping strategies, and to have trained for the situation in advance.

Eye wear

Make sure that you have appropriate eye wear for dealing with challenging light conditions. When buying goggles, if possible, go to a shop on a day when the light is challenging and try them on outside the shop, looking at some snow. What works for one person, may not be suitable for another. Always have your poor visibility goggles in your rucksack so that you can change them during the day if required.

Drag the downhill pole

Become aware of what your uphill pole is doing. Is it dragging on the snow? If it is, lift it off the snow so that it isn't being used as an anchor. This will move the body into a much better position, with more 'C' shape. This will become helpful not only in poor visibility, but in any circumstance. Often skiers say that they are dragging their uphill pole to get a feel for the snow. However, it is much better to feel the snow that is beneath you, that you are about to encounter, rather than feel snow that you have already passed.

This skier (right) is dragging their uphill pole on the snow, only giving them information about the snow and terrain that they have already skied over.

These skiers (below) are dragging their lower pole on the snow, which is giving them information about the snow and terrain below them, and the action is also bringing the body into a good 'C' shape.

POOR VISIBILITY

Dragging the uphill pole can have a detrimental effect on skiing as it tends to bring the balance point over the inside ski and makes it hard to steer the outside ski. However, dragging the downhill pole is an excellent drill for improving balance, and is also a brilliant tool for poor visibility. It provides information about the gradient of the slope and the consistency of the snow, as well as improving balance over the outside ski. Most importantly, it gives information about the snow that is in front of you, rather than the snow that you have already passed.

Pole Drags

Dragging the outside (lower) pole is an excellent drill for developing 'C' shape with the body. It is also an excellent tool when skiing in poor visibility, helping you feel the snow and the gradient. Drag the outside pole on the snow, which will become the lower pole. Imagine that you are trying to draw a circle in the snow with the end of your pole, outside of the line of your skis.

"Dragging my uphill pole was my stabiliser and being from a mountaineering background, I often found myself using it like an ice axe, coming out of a turn pressing on it, willing that it would help ease the unwanted acceleration, not realising that it was in fact a contributing factor. I now focus on keeping my uphill pole off the snow, reminding myself that it is not an ice axe, and drag my lower pole on the snow to help in flat light"

OFF-PISTE PERFORMANCE

Ski by feel

'Ski by feel' is a commonly used phrase but, like all other aspects of skiing, this needs to be practised to be helpful. This involves a huge shift in focus, away from focusing on what we can or can't see, to focusing on what we can feel. All the energy needs to be channelled into feeling the movements that you are making, and feeling what is happening under your skis. Your hip, knee and ankle joints will be constantly bending and stretching to adapt to the changes. What will become apparent is that if you are relaxed these movements can happen automatically. Often when seeing changes in terrain and snow, we tense up and restrict our movements. Relax and the body will work to keep you in balance. The body does not want to fall over!

Eyes closed skiing is an excellent drill for preparing for flat light and poor visibility.

Eyes Closed Skiing

Try traversing across a patch of snow with your eyes closed. Feel every change of terrain and snow under your feet and feel how you adapt with your body to stay in balance. Describe the changes in terrain and snow out loud and your partner can tell you if you are correct, proving that you can 'ski by feel'. When you feel comfortable traversing with your eyes closed, progress by doing some turns on a quiet, gentle piste. Work with a partner who has their eyes open and can shout 'STOP' at any time should there be a hazard or obstacle.

Skiing – a team sport

There will be changes in the way that terrain is skied from person to person skiing within the same group, skiing the same slope, at the same time. This is particularly apparent when skiing powder in narrow places, whether it be in trees or in gullies. The person at the back will be faced with a completely different set of choices to the person at the front.

This difference can be used to help the weaker skiers in your group, by giving them more favourable conditions to ski. For example, in breakable crust, the hardest conditions are for the first person to ski in the snow, as the snow has not been disturbed anywhere. The more the snow is disturbed and broken up, the easier the slope will become. In this situation, the strongest skiers can go first, with the weaker skiers going after, following in the tracks that others have made, who have already broken through the crust.

In powder, this may be giving the weaker skiers in the group the opportunity to go first, to experience feeling the resistance of the snow to help with speed control.

In poor visibility, it is incredibly hard and tiring to be the skier at the front, as there can be virtually no definition. Those that follow will get some definition from watching the skier in front, and therefore an idea of snow type and terrain. If you are following a guide, instructor or friend, recognise this and give them space at the front. They will need to ski much slower than those following. While you are having a pleasant ski behind, they will be working very hard to identify a safe line. When skiing in poor visibility as a group, consider swapping around who goes at the front, to give the leader a rest and divide the hard work.

ADDITIONAL SKILLS

These skills are not essential, but can be helpful in a variety of situations and are beneficial additions to the off-piste skier's tool box. They may give further confidence in places that feel challenging, as well as making descents more efficient. Each of these skills requires familiarisation and practice away from the situation in which they are to be used.

HALF TURNS

These are very similar to turns that are often referred to as garlands, as the tracks left in the snow can look like hanging garland tinsel. Garlands are commonly used by snowboarders, who wish to stay on one edge of the snowboard. Half turns are the motion of doing half a turn, going from travelling in one direction, to travelling down the fall line, to travelling back in the same direction as at the start. When doing half turns the skier will be on one edge the majority of the time, for example, the skier will be on the right-hand edges of the skis, then going on the base of the skis, and then return to the right-hand edges.

1. Initiate the turn (key movement of moving over the skis) and release the edges of the skis.
2. Let the skis come flat and into the fall line.
3. Turn the skis back onto the same edges and return the skis to their initial direction of travel.

Tracks left in the snow by half turns. The skier is only turning to the right, and then back to the fall line, never completing the turn to the left. Notice the difference in snow displacement. The turns on the right-hand side of the photo have very little, whereas the turns on the left-hand side have much more.

OFF-PISTE PERFORMANCE

Skier practising half turns and, as a result, descending diagonally across the slope.

Half turns are a good tool to use when you need to ski across the fall line to get to where you want to go. For example, when faced with a slope of lovely powder that needs to be descended diagonally, integrating half turns into the descent ensures making the best use of the snow and keeps the positive action of the turn going, where side slipping and traversing would be a waste of the snow and lead to a more static performance. Half turns can be incredibly playful, and lots of fun.

Half turns are a terrific tactic for steering away from obstacles which are seen at the last minute, for example, if you spot a rock on the downhill side of a bump. This shouldn't be thought of as a reluctant action, or shying away from the turn, but rather a precise and deliberate action, demonstrating skill and accuracy.

ADDITIONAL SKILLS

Another time when half turns can be deployed is when finding the best snow to ski, which might not always be directly down the fall line. You may need to move around the slope to stay on the preferable aspect. For example, if you are skiing in an area where the best snow is in the shade, the shaded area may go across the fall line. In order to stay in that good snow, you can be creative and incorporate half turns into your descent.

Skiing diagonally across the fall line, completing the turn to the right, and never fully turning to the left.

JUMP TURNS

Jump turns follow the same theme as the ways of turning described earlier. There are two main variations of jump turns, both of which require a high degree of energy and accuracy. You can jump and twist the skis, or jump and change the edges of the skis. The 'jump' element is the same in both, but the turning action differs.

Skiers turning their skis in the air, arguably more for fun than necessity (photos ▼ ▶).

Jumping out of necessity, where the skis need to be brought to the surface of the snow to be able to turn them (photos ▲ ▶).

OFF-PISTE PERFORMANCE

As with twisting and edging the skis when on the snow, think of twisting being at one end of a spectrum and edging at the other, with many possible combinations and blends in between. If we become proficient at both ends of the spectrum, then we will have the skills to vary the movements to achieve the required blend, which depends on the prevailing conditions. A twisting jump will allow the turn to be executed in a very small space, gathering little, if any, speed. An edge change jump needs to be done with speed and requires space. Both are useful whenever the skis feel like they are stuck in the snow and need to be brought to the surface for twisting or edging to occur.

Firstly, let's look at the jumping action on its own as this is the same within both types of turns. Stand on a flat area without skis on.

1. Sink down, flexing ankles, knees and hips.
2. Extend and stretch the ankles, knees and hips, to spring off the snow.
3. Aim to land centred, with the whole foot touching the snow at the same time.
4. Continue to absorb on landing, by bending hips, knees and ankles to make the landing as soft as possible.

The jumping action performed in isolation on a flat area, without skis on.

A common mistake is to try to pull the legs up, rather than push off the snow. It is surprising how little the skis need to leave the snow, the aim is not to get the skis high, merely to push off the snow.

Then practise the same action with skis on.

The skier is pulling their legs up, rather than pushing off the snow. While this might look impressive, it is hard work and makes landing far more challenging and uncomfortable (photo ▶).

Practising the jump action with skis on, aiming for the skis to be parallel to the ground when they are off the snow (photo far ▶).

ADDITIONAL SKILLS

Skier landing from a jump with good 'C' shape to maintain balance over the outside ski.

Next, practise the same action again, but on a slope rather than a flat area. Again, first with skis off, then with skis on. This will focus on the adaptations that need to be made for the gradient of the slope. For a successful and controlled landing, the balance needs to be over the outside (lower) ski to maintain grip.

Push not Pull

This is an exercise to be done at home on solid bathroom scales, to help to get the feeling of pushing off the snow, rather than pulling the knees up. Stand on the scales and note the number. Sink down and push off the scales with both feet, extending the legs as the feet leave the ground. Land centrally, absorbing through the ankles, knees and hips on landing. Note the highest number while doing this. Next, instead of pushing and extending the legs, try pulling your knees towards your chest, then land on the scales; you will notice that the numbers are much higher. Do a few more with the pushing and extending action, aiming to get the numbers as low as possible. The softer the landing, the lower the numbers will be, and the better the action will be for jump turns.

"I felt much greater control on steeper slopes as soon as I made the link between the gradient of slope, body 'C' shape, and landing balanced on my outside ski. The steeper the slope, the greater 'C' shape required, much against my natural instinct of wanting to lean into the hill. Simply focusing on lifting my uphill hand away from the slope helped me to achieve this, particularly during the landing phase of a jump turn."

OFF-PISTE PERFORMANCE

Twist jump

This is the action of twisting in the air. The twisting is the same action as mentioned earlier in the book, only this time it is being done in the air. The good news is that there is no need to twist the skis 180 degrees. Wherever the skis land, the twisting action can, and should, continue on the snow, until the skis are perpendicular to the slope.

As with the jumping action in isolation, it is recommended to practise this action without skis on, first on the flat and then on a slope. Then, when comfortable and fluid with the motion, try it with skis on.

Practising a twisting jump turn without skis on (photos ▶ ▲).

Checking that the backs of the skis are parallel, and not diverging, before committing to a jump turn (photo ▼).

The great thing about twisting jump turns is that much of the success comes from preparation, which is all done when stationary.

1. Stand with the skis perpendicular to the slope, hip width apart.
2. Check that the skis are parallel (look at the backs too). Any divergence in the skis will make the turn harder. However, starting with a very small convergence shape will make it slightly easier to turn the skis, as you've already started to turn the upper ski while on the ground.
3. Place the downhill ski pole near the back binding. This will help to rotate the upper body down the mountain and leave the area where the skis are going to twist clear from obstructions.
4. The uphill pole should be placed the same distance in front, for stability.
5. Sink down at least once, or more times to give a better bounce if needed.
6. Extend the legs as you push upwards, away from the snow.

ADDITIONAL SKILLS

Well prepared for a jump turn. This is the starting position, and it is also the finish position. Aim to finish the turn in a position ready to start the next turn.

7. Twist the skis as they come off the surface of the snow.
8. Land balanced, centred over the outside (lower) ski.
9. Continue the turn on the snow, if required to control speed.

Twisting jump turns are often used on steep terrain, but they do not need to be, as shown in the earlier section on steep skiing. It uses less energy to turn the skis on the snow than in the air. As a guideline, a twisting jump turn is most applicable when you'd like to do a twist for speed control reasons but the skis are 'in' the snow, rather than 'on' the snow. For example, on a narrow, steep section when the skis are deep in the snow and the skis need to be brought to the surface.

Practising a twisting jump turn off-piste, in easy-angled terrain.

OFF-PISTE PERFORMANCE

Edge jump
This is the action of changing the edges of the skis looked at in the turning chapter, but doing it in the air. An element of rotation will take place as this happens, but the goal is to change the edge of the skis.

Again, the first practice should be without skis on, on a flat area. This practice is harder to do than for the twisting turns, and poles may need to be used to aid balance. Notice how the majority of the practice is the same as for the twist jump turn, apart from one action, which is the rolling of the foot rather than a twist.

1. Stand with the feet hip width apart, and balanced on the edges of the boots.
2. Sink down.
3. Extend the legs as you push upwards, away from the snow.
4. Change the edge of the boots as they come off the surface of the snow.
5. Land on the opposite edges of the boots.

Practising edge changes in the air, without skis on.

Then move to practise with skis on, in a turn. An element of speed is needed for this to be successful, which is the key difference to the twisting jump turns, along with the turning area being much greater.

1. Let the skis pick up some momentum.
2. Sink down.
3. Extend the legs as you push upwards, away from the snow.
4. Change the edge of the skis as they come off the surface of the snow. The output from this will be that the skis start to turn.
5. Land balanced, centred over the outside ski.

(See photo sequence on opposite page.)

Skier uses edge jump turns off-piste to get the skis out of the heavy snow.

Edge jump turns are most useful when the skis are 'in' the snow, rather than 'on' the snow. They help when it's challenging to turn, an element of momentum is required to get through the snow, and an edged ski is required to push snow out of the way, for example in heavy snow or breakable crust.

Similar to the half turns, edge jump turns can feel fun and playful, particularly in chopped-up powder and are often done for sheer enjoyment and creativity rather than because of a particular snow type or terrain feature.

ADDITIONAL SKILLS

Practising edge jump turns on the piste.

When unsure of the precise consistency of the snow and you are apprehensive about how easy it will be to turn, try starting off with an edge jump turn. This can give a more successful start to the descent, and the amount of jump can then be dialled back as you become more familiar with, and confident about, the consistency of the snow.

Jump turns, both twisting and edging, and all the drills in the lead up, are excellent drills. Even if you never have any intention of doing a jump turn, they can help significantly with enhancing all of the key movements and becoming a better all-round off-piste skier.

"My heart sank when the instructor said that we'd be practising jump turns. I can't do them, and I have no intention of ever doing one. However, as the practice session was broken down into progressive bite size chunks, I engaged and participated in the drills. I still backed away from practising the whole jump turn but I was amazed by my progress in skiing narrow, steep sections off-piste. I had become a much springier skier as a result of all the jumping drills, something I had never thought I would become. I now regularly practise jump turn drills, even though I still have no intention of doing a jump turn, as it makes me use a much greater range of movement and become springier on my skis."

OFF-PISTE PERFORMANCE

DOUBLE POLE PLANT

A double pole plant can be used to aid balance and give additional spring in any situation but is most useful when aiming to turn in a small space or on steep terrain, using a twisting action either on the snow or with a jump.

1. Place the downhill pole behind you, near the back of your binding.
2. Place the uphill pole in front of you, towards the tips of your skis. Experiment with the placement of this pole. Placing it a similar distance in front of your body to the distance the downhill pole is behind, generally feels most balanced.
3. Push off both poles as you initiate the turn.

Using a double pole plant on steeper terrain.

BATON RAMASSE

This technique originated from the French technique 'piolet ramasse' which is a technique used in mountaineering involving an ice axe, as opposed to ski poles. Baton ramasse is good for increasing stability when side stepping to manoeuvre on steeper ground or to get around an obstacle. It is often used when entering a steep couloir.

1. Hold ski poles horizontally, at belly button height.
2. Place one hand near the baskets and the other hand near the grips.
3. Have the basket ends of the poles in contact with the slope on the uphill side.
4. Keep weight over the skis and keep the body upright, using the poles for stability and balance, but avoid pressing down on them for support.
5. Side step downhill, either moving the feet or the poles, but not both at the same time.

It is not advisable to use this technique when side slipping, only side stepping, as the skis are likely to slide out from underneath the body due to the increased momentum, resulting in a loss of stability.

Increasing stability using baton ramasse on steeper ground.

ADDITIONAL SKILLS

SMALL DROPS

Some may gulp at the inclusion of this and may quickly flip past, thinking that this section is not for them. Please keep reading; you are exactly who it is for. There is huge merit to practising having your skis in the air and becoming familiar with staying in balance while 'dropping' off small lips. Firstly, if you practise with skis in the air, it's less of a surprise if they accidentally end up being there, and you are more likely to be able to react and adjust to stay in balance. Secondly, being able to negotiate small drops often gives access to fabulous off-piste terrain, which might otherwise have to be avoided. You may find yourself standing at the top of a bowl getting increasingly nervous about the entry which is over an edge. The increase in tension will impact the whole descent. Conversely, spend time practising going over little edges and drops, and you will be stood at the top, barely noticing the entry, but able to focus on the delightful powder in the bowl below. Search out little drops in safe places and have fun practising going over them.

Wind lips can form at the top of bowls and corries and being able to pass them confidently will aid the whole descent (photo ▼).

A small wind feature, ideal for practising on (photo ▶).

Enjoying playing on a wee drop, primarily for fun, but also for practice. (photos ▲ ▶).

Leaving the ground

Always check the landing before leaving the ground. Check for any obstacles such as trees and rocks. Make a mental note of the gradient and snow type of the landing area, being cautious of landing on flat ground or a firm surface. You will need to adapt your landing depending on the gradient as well as the softness and depth of the snow. After making these observations, select where you wish to pass through the edge. You can mark the area with a line in the snow or pick a stationary landmark on the horizon.

The group is checking out the landing and discussing which line they will take.

There are two choices on leaving the ground: to 'pop' or to 'drop'. If you decide that you want to travel further and higher in the air, then you may wish to 'pop' at the lip, which will feel like taking off. This is done by extending the legs, as described in the jumping section. If you would like to limit the time and distance travelled in the air, then it is possible to 'drop', which means going off the lip in a centred and balanced position, doing no additional movements on take-off. In both circumstances keep looking ahead, not at your feet.

Landing

Be prepared for landing by continuing to focus ahead and feeling stable through your core. When your skis touch the snow, flex from the hips, knees and ankles to absorb the landing. Landing in deep snow requires more focus

Dropping off a small wind lip. The skier is in a flexed position ready to absorb the landing.

ADDITIONAL SKILLS

This skier is slightly back from a centred position while in the air. This is appropriate for this situation, as they need to keep the tips of the skis out of the snow, as they are about to land in deep powder. They landed successfully!

on the heels to keep the fronts of the skis out of the snow, while firmer snow requires a landing central on the skis, remembering both shin and heel.

When landing in the fall line, the weight should be spread equally over both skis. However, you don't always need to land directly down the fall line. Depending on the nature of the slope, it can be possible to take a line which lands perpendicular to the hill. This can be far less intimidating as it will feel like you are going across, rather than down the slope, and the acceleration will be less. If you decide to do this, remember to land balanced over the lower ski, with good 'C' shape to avoid falling into the slope.

Taking a line more perpendicular to the slope to have less acceleration and maintaining a good 'C' shape on landing to remain balanced over the lower ski.

DOWNHILL KICK TURNS

Downhill kick turns should be reserved for use on low-angled terrain where the consequence of getting the turn wrong is minimal and would not result in a slide. They are most useful in breakable crust when the risk of injury through turning is high.

1. Stand perpendicular to the slope, with both skis pointing the same way. Create a solid platform by stamping down the snow.
2. Place poles out of the way but in a position that assists with balance.
3. Balance on the upper ski.
4. Turn the lower ski to face the opposite direction. Place it parallel to the upper ski with the boots as close together as possible.
5. Balance on the lower ski (and use poles to aid balance).
6. Turn the upper ski around to match the lower ski.

(See photo sequence at top of opposite page.)

In soft snow, it is possible to do a variation which requires less flexibility.

1. Stand perpendicular to the slope, with both skis pointing the same way. Create a solid platform by stamping down the snow.
2. Place poles out of the way but in a position to assist with balance.
3. Turn the lower ski to face down the fall line and at right angles to the upper ski. Insert the tail into the snow, as far as it can go, ideally up to the back of the binding.
4. Bring the upper ski around, passing underneath the ski that is inserted into the snow, to become the lower ski.
5. Push forward slightly on the new lower ski and pivot the upper ski to come parallel to the lower ski. The tail of the ski will come free from the snow with a small movement forward.

(See photo sequence at bottom of opposite page.)

> ❗ A downhill kick turn should not be used on steep slopes. It is a delicate manoeuvre, requiring good balance and core strength. The consequence of getting it wrong is serious, with the potential for a head-first slide down the slope. On steep terrain, plan ahead and aim to stop with space in front of you to do the next turn. If you find yourself stationary, facing the wrong direction, it is safer to move to a place where you can turn rather than do a downhill kick turn. This may be by side slipping down or traversing across, but remember you can also side step up, or traverse backwards, to create space in front of you to turn.

ADDITIONAL SKILLS

Demonstrating a downhill kick turn.

Demonstrating a variation on the downhill kick turn, which works in softer snow conditions.

COMMONLY ASKED QUESTIONS

Focused; ready to make the most of the untracked powder conditions (photo ▲).

The answer to most of these questions is 'it depends', as so often the answer will depend on the many variables of the ever-changing off-piste environment. Variables such as the level of skier, the desired speed of travel, the type of snow and the terrain will all influence the answer. What is correct for one person in one situation, might not work for someone else in the same situation. What works for one person one day, might not work for the same person on a different day. The answers here give simple guidance to help you to find the solution to your question in any given situation.

Where should the upper body face?

The upper body should face the direction of momentum. When travelling across the mountain, the body should face across the mountain. When travelling down the mountain, the upper body should face down the mountain. Normally this means that in shorter turns, like in trees or couloirs, the body will face down the slope as the direction of momentum is down the hill. In longer turns that come perpendicular to the fall line, the body will face across the slope as the direction of momentum is across the slope.

Fresh tracks in soft snow with snow displacement clearly visible around the turns (photo ◄).

In both situations, aligning the upper body with the direction of momentum will help to maintain balance and aid rotation. If you try to face down the mountain when travelling across it, stability will feel compromised and the body will feel twisted. Try absorbing a bump in this position and it is likely to

OFF PISTE PERFORMANCE

Upper body facing across the hill, as momentum is going across the hill.

be with limited success. Turn the body in line with the direction of travel and you will feel stable and free to bend and stretch. Skiing in a narrow corridor feels very difficult if the whole body turns from side to side. In this situation, it's better to let the upper body face downhill, in the direction of momentum, and for the skis to turn independently of the upper body.

Upper body facing down the hill, as momentum is going down the hill.

"I prefer to do fast, longer turns. For a long time, I battled to keep my body facing down the hill when doing them, always feeling slightly awkward. Once I knew it was 'ok' to let my body face where I was going (across the slope) I instantly felt more stable and balanced and could go even faster."

Refer to drill 'Poles Downhill' (page 86) in the section on Twisting to help with keeping the body facing downhill while doing shorter turns.

How far apart should my skis be?

Having the skis hip width apart will provide a good stable platform, which aids bending and stretching. This is a good position to work from. However, this needs to be varied depending on the individual, the skis being used, the snow, the speed and the terrain. Think of a downhill racer and a mogul skier. The downhill racer will have the skis further apart and the mogul skier will have the skis closer together, because they are in different situations, on different equipment, and trying to achieve different things. When travelling

COMMONLY ASKED QUESTIONS

Different skiers, in different terrain, with different widths of stance. The common theme is that they are all having fun and enjoying their turns.

at higher speeds, greater stability is gained with a wider stance. If the skis are too close together it is harder to balance. If the skis are too far apart it can feel strenuous and it is harder to make efficient and simultaneous edge changes. The key is to adapt your stance throughout the day in order to keep the strength in your legs for when you need it.

How do I stop accelerating out of the turn?

Think of the acceleration out of the end of the turn as the symptom, not the cause. The cause is likely to be one of two things, which both relate back to the key movements. It may be because you are not balanced on the outside ski in the later stages of the turn. This causes the skier's weight to fall to the inside of the turn, which causes acceleration and a loss of control. This can be helped by simply placing the hand on the outside knee through the turn, this will bring the balance back over the outside ski. This drill was described in the section on balancing over the outside ski. It is repeated here, but this time being done off-piste, incorporated into the skiing, rather than as a drill.

Placing a hand on the outside knee to control speed through the end of the turn.

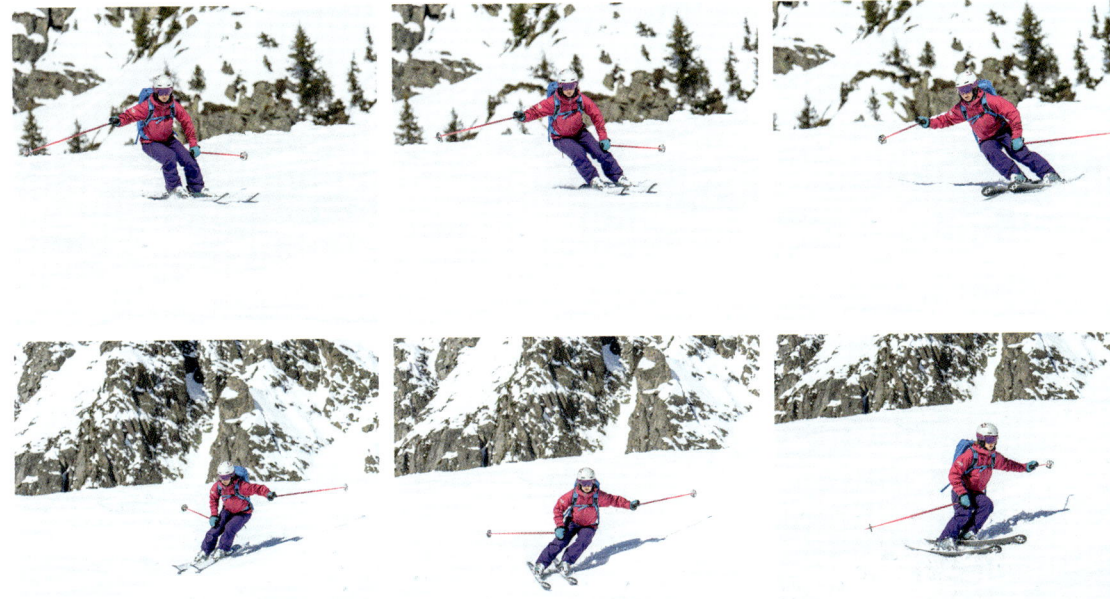

169

The acceleration may also occur because you have not moved forward into the turn, resulting in the skis being ahead of the hips in the fall line, again causing an acceleration and a loss of control. This loss of control results in the skier not being able to turn the skis as effectively through the end of the turn as they may desire.

> Refer to the drills for balancing over the outside ski and moving forward into the turn (pages 66 - 78).

Putting the hand towards, but not on, the knee, aiding balance over the outside ski.

How do I prevent myself from leaning back?

This is very similar to feeling the acceleration out of the end of the turn, and the two normally go hand in hand. Leaning back is the symptom not the cause. If thought of as 'leaning back' it's very difficult to solve. Instead, think of leaning back as the symptom of either not being balanced over the outside ski, or not having moved forward into the turn. When you feel this happening, focus on the solution, something that you know helps you to move forward into the next turn or something that helps you balance better over the outside ski, both of which will have a positive influence on the performance. For example, this could be simply saying 'hip' to remind you to move forward into the turn, or saying 'hand' to bring your hand towards your knee and improve balance over the outside ski.

> Refer to the drills for balancing over the outside ski and moving forward into the turn (pages 66 - 78).

> "I used to think I was leaning back, but in fact, I was forgetting to move forward"

How much weight should I have on each ski?

It depends. Firstly, try to think of how you balance across the two skis, rather than how much weight should be on each ski. It's a subtle but significant difference. If we think of 'weight' then there is a tendency to end up 'pressing' on the skis, which in soft snow can cause them to sink.

When travelling straight down a slope, you will balance equally between the two skis. If you are traversing across the slope, you need to balance more on the lower ski. Therefore, the further around the corner you come when turning, the more you need to balance on the outside ski, which becomes the lower ski at the end of the turn.

In powder snow, you might take a line directly down the fall line, in which case the balance will be more equal over both skis. However, unless going straight down the fall line, you should be more dominant on the outside ski to stay in balance, even if the balance is split 51%, 49%.

COMMONLY ASKED QUESTIONS

Skiers often ski further around the corner to reduce speed, particularly on steep ground. This is when it's key to remember to stay balanced over the outside ski.

Refer to the myths of powder skiing (page 99).

💡 *"For years I have thought I needed to do more with my inside ski. But by becoming more balanced on my outside ski, my inside ski is now doing more and I am able to get both skis to do the same thing at the same time."*

Why are my skis clicking together at the back?

If you hear skis clicking at the back when turning, look at the backs of your skis. You will probably see scratches on the back of them where they have been clicking together. This occurs because the skis aren't parallel, but in fact diverging. You can get away with this in many situations, but it becomes a real problem in crust as it is difficult to control speed and line.

Refer to the section on Perfectly Parallel in Crust (page 116).

Scratches on the back of skis, due to the two skis touching each other through the turn. They could also be due to doing tricks in the park – but you will probably know which has caused them!

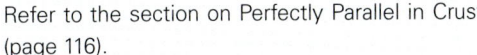

Why do I fall over off-piste?

There are three main technical reasons why skiers fall over off-piste.
1. The skier is not balanced over the outside ski.
2. The skier has not moved forward into the turn.
3. The skier has not used appropriate bending and stretching.

The end result of all of these is that the skier finds themselves out of balance and falling, either into the hill, backwards, or over the front of the skis. Of course, there are other reasons, such as hitting a rock or getting skis crossed, but if you start observing yourself and other skiers, you'll see that primarily, at all levels of skiing, falling will be down to one of these three reasons.

The skier has lost balance to the inside of the turn (uphill) due to not balancing effectively on the outside ski through the whole turn (photo ▼).

The skier is losing balance over the front of the skis, due to limited use of bending and stretching (photo ▶).

OFF-PISTE PERFORMANCE

Therefore, by developing the key movements, you will be less likely to fall over. It is ok to fall over, but try to use it as a positive 'training moment' and recognise why there was a loss of balance, so that a positive response can be developed if the same loss of balance is felt again.

Refer to all of the Key Movements (page 62). Select one significant word that helps you to bring about a positive response to enhance each key movement. If you feel yourself losing balance for one of the three reasons above, say the relevant key word out loud. For example, if you find that you often lose balance over the front of skis in powder, this is most likely due to ineffective use of bending and stretching. Say to yourself "bend" as you feel the skis start to decelerate to bring about a positive response and regain balance.

How do I stop myself from snowploughing when I don't want to?

Firstly, check that you are sure that you don't want to be snowploughing, as it is an essential skill. There are places where snowploughing is the most effective way to turn, for example, in any situation where snow needs to be pushed out of the way, particularly when travelling at slow speeds.

If you are snowploughing when you don't want to, or need to, it is most likely because the uphill ski has started to turn, while you are still balanced on the lower ski.

These skiers have started to turn their uphill ski, while still being balanced on the lower one, hence creating a wedge shape with their skis.

The skier is balanced over the lower ski, as they have started to turn the uphill ski, hence creating a snowplough.

COMMONLY ASKED QUESTIONS

The skier is now balancing on the uphill (new outside) ski before the turn is initiated, making it impossible for the skis to form a snowplough shape. In this photo, the lower ski is lifted off the snow to highlight that the balance has been transferred. The aim is for the balance to be transferred, not for the ski to be lifted.

Notice that there isn't a cross beside these photos. It's not wrong, but if you want to avoid going into a snowplough, the balance needs to be transferred from the lower ski (old outside ski) to the upper ski (new outside ski) before the turn, when the skis are perpendicular to the slope. This is sometimes referred to as making an early transition from one ski to the other.

Refer to sections on Snowploughing (page 56), Edging (page 87) and Heavy Snow (page 108).

How do I prevent the backs of my skis from catching in the snow as I turn?

The backs of the skis catch because there is more weight on the backs of the skis than the fronts. It normally becomes more apparent in snow that the skis are in, rather than on. This can be solved by exaggerating the move forward into the turn. As you do this, think of lightening the backs of the skis.

Refer to the key movement of Moving Forward into the Turn (page 73) and look specifically at the Toe on the Snow drill (page 80).

These skiers will feel the back of their ski catching because the front of the ski is lifted, resulting in the back of the ski digging into the snow.

Practise the Toe on the Snow drill to help keep 'toes on the snow', to avoid the skis catching at the back.

OFF-PISTE PERFORMANCE

These skiers have used their lower leg as a 'brake' to slow them as they come out of the turn. These images don't have a cross through them, because they are not wrong, but controlling speed can be done better, by either pushing both legs or turning up the hill to slow down.

Is it a problem having a straight lower leg?

It can be. The lower leg tends to straighten because it is stretched out at the end of the turn to slow speed, acting as a brake. When the goal is to slow down and this is achieved, this is not necessarily a bad thing. However, travelling across a slope with a straight lower leg means that bending and stretching will be ineffective, and balance may be compromised.

To avoid having a straight lower leg, try using the hill more to control speed, by continuing to steer the skis around the curve until the desired speed is reached. Another solution is to think of both legs acting as a brake, rather than just one, actively scraping the snow with both skis to control speed.

This skier has controlled their speed by pushing snow with both skis and as a result, both legs stay flexed and ready to absorb whatever terrain comes next. Notice the spray of snow coming off both the inside and outside ski.

Refer to the scrubbing action described for controlling speed on paths (page 141) and ensure that this is done with both skis.

I ski well on-piste but struggle off-piste. Why might this be?

This could be down to under-exaggerated key movements. All of the key movements have a place on piste, but the problem is that you can get away without doing them. This is much less true when skiing off-piste. Spend time on piste exaggerating the key movements to ensure that they are always present in your skiing.

It could also be related to one of the other components, such as physical, psychological or equipment. Are your skis suitable for going off-piste? Are you physically prepared for going off-piste? Do you find yourself phased by the lack of marker poles?

One of the psychological implications of skiing off-piste in powder is that sometimes we can't see our skis, something that is rare when skiing on piste. Spend some time skiing on piste, checking that you are not looking at your skis, but looking further ahead, to get used to this sensation.

Patience can also be key. The skis can take a little longer to respond to the movements we make when they are in the snow, rather than on the surface. To help become more patient, try counting 'turn 1,2,3, turn, 1,2,3', with the 1,2,3 being points on the curve around the turn.

Due to the other environmental factors when skiing off-piste, like rocks, trees and lack of defined boundaries, we can find it hard to know where to focus our attention. It's important to only focus on one thing at a time, so as not to become overloaded with thoughts and information. The key is finding the one factor that will have the greatest positive influence on your skiing in any given situation, and this is where the role of a coach may come in. It could be as simple as focusing on something like breathing.

> "I'm a strong piste skier and have spent vast amounts of time refining my technique, however, I struggled when I stepped the other side of the marker poles. I am a swimmer and I recently made a transition from pool swimming to open water swimming. Initially, I found the open water uncomfortable. It was clearly evident that I needed to focus on my breathing to remain calm in the open water. Focusing on breathing when skiing was less obvious to me and I hadn't considered it until my coach suggested trying it. I then realised that I might even have been holding my breath when I went off-piste! I now solely focus on smooth continual breaths, timed with my turns, and I find my strong piste performance comes with me into the off-piste"

Refer to all the Key Movements (page 61) and look at all the other components in the Preparation section (page 23).

OFF-PISTE PERFORMANCE

What are compression turns?
Compression turns are when the edges of the skis are changed in a low, flexed position, most often used when skiing bumps. This book has steered away from labelling types of turns, but instead given key movements and different ways of turning, which can be varied to give infinite turning outcomes. Think of turns like snowflakes, no two are ever the same. The blend of movements in each turn will be different, however slight or great. Take a compression turn for example, rather than view the turn as being possible with flexed legs or straight legs, a turn can be done with the legs in any position between the two extremes, each giving a subtly different outcome.

I find that my pole plant drags me back. What should I do?
The pole plant should be viewed as the icing on the cake, not essential. Done well, a pole plant can aid balance and stability, done poorly it can hinder performance. If you find that the pole plant is hindering your performance, firstly try skiing without doing a pole plant, focusing on one of the key movements and keeping the hands still and uninvolved in the action of the rest of the body.

Pole Balance
Ski with your pole balanced on the back of your wrists. This encourages the hands into a still and stable position to remove them from the action of the rest of the body.

Pole Balance drill to help keep the hands still to aid balance.

When you try bringing the pole plant back into your skiing make the action small and subtle, using mostly the wrist. Plant your pole and remember to take it with you. If you leave the pole in the snow, this hand will end up behind you, twisting the body into the hill.

💡 "My mantra became 'plant and lift' as I needed a trigger word to remind me to take my pole with me after planting it. Before, my pole plant felt like a hassle and a hindrance, now it feels helpful."

Refer to the Steep section to learn about pole planting near the back of the bindings (page 121).

COMMONLY ASKED QUESTIONS

How far ahead should I look when skiing off-piste?

The primary focus should be on looking at the exit of the turn, but the wider field of vision will take in the terrain that is further ahead; very similar to driving. Look too far ahead and your connection with the skis and feet will be lost. Look down too much and you'll not see what is coming up.

Looking at the exit of the turn has many positive outcomes. It helps with the turn initiation and it also helps psychologically as you are telling yourself that the turn has been completed and are visualising the line in the snow where the turn will occur. Rather than thinking about doing the turn, you are telling yourself that you have done it. The skis may still be finishing one turn, but the mind and body have already engaged in the next one, resulting in the most fabulous sensation of rhythmical swoopy turns, like a pendulum going from side to side.

Refer to the Physical section (page 25) and notice how the mountain biker is looking at the exit of the corner. Where to look is transferable from many other sports.

Looking at the exit of the turn. Although you can't see the eyes, notice that the head is slightly turned to focus on the point where the skis will exit from the turn.

Why do I find the first turn so difficult?

This is no surprise as for every pitch that is skied, the first turn is only practised once, whereas all the others are practised hundreds of times within the one run. Take time to practise the first turn repeatedly. Have a run where you practise the first turn, stop and practise it again, and repeat until the first turn has been practised hundreds of times. This is an ideal thing to do on a bad weather day, or when you only have a small patch of snow to practise on.

The key to executing a good first turn is momentum. This can either be the momentum of the skis, or the momentum of the body if it's not possible to get the skis moving first. If there is space to start traversing across the hill, the first turn is generally easier. However, take this space away and it becomes more challenging. In this case, try starting with a side slip before doing the first turn. Practising from stationary is the hardest, as in this case the momentum needs to be generated by moving forward into the turn before the skis move anywhere.

Refer to Moving Forward into the Turn (page 73).

Practising the first turn from stationary repeatedly is key to being able to execute a good first turn.

My technique is fine but I struggle psychologically. What can I do to help?

Have a strong positive technical focus that you have practised and rehearsed many times in less challenging situations, so that you know you ski better when thinking of it. Focus on the positive aspects of your skiing, rather than what needs to be improved. Saying the focus out loud helps to avoid any other distractions coming in. It can be as simple as saying 'hip' before you commit to the turn, as a reminder to move the hip across the skis. Mental rehearsal will also help with this, either feeling yourself doing the actions or visualising yourself skiing the slope successfully.

Describe your Skiing

Select a word that describes how you'd like to see yourself ski. Words like flowing, rhythmical, swoopy, strong, aggressive, powerful, light, accurate, bouncy will all work well and will all have different outcomes. Try it and see. It's amazing how a group can do this drill, keep the words secret, and when you watch each individual ski, you can have a pretty good guess as to what word each person chose.

Derek Tate's book *Ski Steps to Training the Mind* is an excellent resource for skiers who want to develop the psychological component.

What is the main difference between good skiers and very good skiers?

The main difference between good and very good skiers is their skill level at balancing. That is what we are constantly doing when skiing off-piste; balancing. We adjust balance over the outside ski, we adjust balance by bending and stretching, and we adjust balance back and forwards. A good skier can do this so quickly that it looks deceptively like they are always in balance. This is a myth. What they are doing is constantly making small and subtle adjustments to remain in balance. They are constantly balancing. A less good skier is doing the same thing, only at a slower speed and a more conscious level. They may not be able to make the adjustments as quickly, so a loss of balance results in a fall. Through losing balance, and reflecting on why, you will become better at regaining balance. With time and practice these responses will become quicker and more intuitive.

Enjoying the powder, while being well balanced, ready to bend and flex to deal with the underlying uneven terrain.

Striving to get maximum enjoyment from every turn on Ben Hope in sublime Scottish conditions.
Di Gilbert

INDEX

A
Aeroplane Arms, drill 67

B
balancing over the outside ski 62
Barriers, drill 136
baskets, ski pole 36
baton ramasse 160
BeFit app 26
bending and stretching 68
Big Toe, Little Toe, drill 87
bindings 32
body, facing which way 167
boots 31
boots, contact points 70
Boots Undone, drill 117
bounce, powder 103
brakes 33
bumps 130

C
carving 87
catching, back of skis 173
Central Twist, drill 136
centred, on skis 70
chopped-up powder 105
clicking, back of skis 171
clothing 38
components of performance 23
compression turns 176
concave slopes 129
conditions, changing 39
convex slopes 127
crust 114, 145
curve / 'C' shape 65

D
Dancing, drill 84
DIN setting 33
Diving In, drill 76
double pole plant 160
downhill kick turns 164
drills 18, 19
drops, small 161

E
Edge Early - Both Skis, drill 112
Edge Early - One Ski, drill 110
edge jump turns 158
edges, sharpening 30
edging 81, 87
edging and twisting, blending 102
environmental factors 38
equipment 27
extension and flexion 68
Eyes Closed Skiing, drill 150

F
fall, causes of 171
fall, getting up from 48
fall line 47
firm snow 92
flat light 147
flexion and extension 68
Flex or Face Plant, drill 73
floating, skis 100
Flotation, drill 101
flowing performance 27

G
goggles 36
goggles, poor visibility 148
golf-ball snow 104
gouges, filling 30
grades, off-piste skiing 21
group, skiing in 150
gullies, narrow 137, 145

H
half turns 151
Hand Inside, drill 89
Hand on Knee, drill 66
hard-packed snow 92
heavy snow 108
heel catch 79
helmets 36

I
icy snow 97
inside ski 63
itinerary runs 22

J
juddering, skis 93
jump turns 153
jump turns, edge 158
jump turns, twist 156

K
key movements 61
kick turns, downhill 164

L
leaning back, preventing 170
length, ski 28
Little Edge, Lots of Edge, drill 90
Lots of Turns, drill 124
lower leg, straight 174
lower ski 63

M
micro aspects 113
moguls 130
movements, key 61
movement skills 51
moving forward into the turn 73

N
narrow terrain 134, 144
No Tracks, drill 84

O
outside ski 63
outside ski, balancing over 62

P
Parallel Poles, drill 68
parallel skis 116
paths 141
performance, components of 23
physical preparation 25
Pole Balance, drill 176
Pole Drags, drill 149
Pole on Hips, drill 78
pole plant, double 160
pole plant, narrow terrain 135
pole plant, problems 176
pole plant, steep ground 121
Poles Downhill, drill 86
poles 35

INDEX

poor visibility 147
powder 99, 143, 144
powder, chopped-up 105
practice 42
preparation 23
pressure, applying and managing 90
probes 37
psychological preparation 26
Pull Over, drill 107
Push not Pull, drill 155
putting skis on 44

R
Races, drill 55
radius, ski 28
rain runnels 118
ramp angle 34
repetition 42
ridges, narrow 137
rocker, ski 28
rucksacks 37

S
safety 20
sastrugi 118
scrubbing speed 141
servicing, ski 29
shovels 37
side slipping 53
side stepping 52
sit down turn 50
ski boots 31
ski design, history of 82
skiing by feel 150
skills, movement 51
skills, static 43

skis, catching back of 173
skis, choice 27, 29
skis, clicking at back 171
skis, distance apart 168
Skis in the Air, drill 85
skis, putting on 44
skis, taking off 46
skis, weight on 170
Slide on a Line, drill 55
slopes, concave 129
slopes, convex 127
snowploughing 56
Snowploughing, drill 57
snow, types of 91
speed, scrubbing 141
spring snow 95
Squats in Bumps, drill 72
Squats on Skis, drill 71
static skills 43
steep skiing, history 124
steep terrain 120, 143
Step by Feel, drill 53
stiffness, ski 28
straight lower leg 174
straps, ski pole 36
Strava 21
stretching and bending 68
Superman, drill 77

T
tactical preparation 23
taking skis off 46
technical preparation 23
terrain variations 119
tips level 106

Tips Level, drill 106
Toe on the Snow, drill 80
Tracks, drill 88
training 42
transceivers 37
traversing 58
trees 138
Turn in a Box, drill 123
turning 81
turn, moving forward in 73
turn, compression 176
turn, sit down 50
turn, stop accelerating out of 169
Turn, Turn, Turn, drill 103
twisting 81, 83
twisting and edging, blending 102
twisting jump turns 156
Twist on a Line, drill 85

U
upper ski 63

V
Vamos 21
variations, terrain 119
Vary the Turns, drill 128
visibility, poor 147

W
warming up 40
waxing, ski 31
width, ski 27
wind affected snow 104

As you continue to develop your off-piste performance remember having fun is very important and smiling can go a long way to help performance.